Henri Stierlin

Photographs: Anne and Henri Stierlin

THE MAYA

Palaces and pyramids
of the rainforest

TASCHEN

Köln London Los Angeles Madrid Paris Tokyo

Front cover
Temple I, Tikal, seventh century A.D.
© Photo: Maximilien Bruggmann

Back cover
Palace of the Governor, Uxmal, ninth
century A.D.
© Drawing: Alberto Berengo Gardin

Page 3
Sculpted jade tablet, part of the
treasure found in the crypt of the
Pyramid of the Inscriptions at
Palenque. Dating from before A. D.
675, it shows a man in ceremonial attire
with feather headdress (Mexico City,
Museo Nacional de Antropología).

Page 5
Stela 4 from Machaquila shows a high-
ranking Mayan dignitary wearing ritual
headdress and carrying a small sceptre
in the shape of a man. The Inscription
dates it to A. D. 820 (Guatemala City,
Museo Nacional de Arqueología y
Etnología).

About the author and editor:
Henri Stierlin, born in 1928, studied
at the universities of Lausanne and
Zurich before beginning his career as
a journalist. In 1948 he published his
first articles on art history and made
numerous radio and television pro-
grammes on the history of civilization.
The 16-volume work *Architecture
Universelle*, Éditions de l'Office du
Livre, was published between 1964 and
1972 under Stierlin's direction. He has
also published *The Art of the Maya*,
New York, 1981.

© 2004 TASCHEN GmbH
Hohenzollernring 53, D-50672 Köln
www.taschen.com

Editor-in-chief: Angelika Taschen, Cologne
Edited by Susanne Klinkhamels, Cologne
Co-edited by Caroline Keller, Cologne
Design and layout: Marion Hauff, Milan
Cover design: Catinka Keul, Cologne
English translation: Suzanne Bosman, London

Printed in China
ISBN 3-8228-1241-2

Contents

Introduction

The Maya enter History

The authority of a lord of the jungle
A high-ranking Mayan dignitary in state apparel, wearing a turban-like head-dress, a thick coiled neckscarf and a nuff-like object on his right wrist. The lofty, concentrated expression, the introspective gaze, and the ritual scarring on the cheek give the face a truly Mayan character. Dating from the Classic period, this work in hollow clay from Simojovel (Chiapas), not far from Palenque, is around 50 cm high. (Mexico City, National Museum of Anthropology)

The Maya civilization – the most advanced of the evolved civilizations of Mesoamerica – produced a powerful, grandiose architecture. Dozens of cities and hundreds of monuments are scattered through the huge tropical forest of Guatemala, Honduras, Belize and Mexico, and the scrublands of Yucatán.

Between the beginning of the modern era and the twelfth century, the Mayan tribes created a large number of striking buildings in Quintana Roo, Campeche, Chiapas, the Petén and on the high lands of the volcanic *sierra* of Guatemala. This legacy, now being excavated, studied and restored by teams of local archaeologists and by specialists sent by major American and European universities, offers evidence of the extraordinary dynamism of Amerindian societies. It illustrates the superlative artistic sensibility that flourished in the New World at a time when Europe was witnessing the flowering of Roman civilization, the great invasions and the subsequent birth of the Middle Ages.

But the exceptional nature of the art and architecture of the Pre-Columbians resides in a paradoxical fact, which confounds historians and anthropologists alike. These works were conceived by civilizations that had no contact whatever with the Ancient World. Before the Spanish conquest, the peoples of Mesoamerica had been influenced neither by western civilizations nor by those of the Far East. All connections, all relations between the inhabitants of Europe and Asia and the Amerindian peoples had been severed before the dawn of the Neolithic era.

The human settlement of the American continent is relatively recent: man arrived in the New World towards the end of the Paleolithic era. Between 70 000 and 10 000 B.C., during the last period of glaciations, known as the Würm (or in the U.S. as the Wisconsin glaciations), successive waves of nomadic Siberian hunters made their way into Alaska.

The lowering of the sea-level due to the accumulation of glaciers in the Arctic and Antarctic regions allowed these hunter-gatherers to cross by land between Asia and America. A land bridge formed in the region now occupied by the Bering Strait and the Aleutian archipelago. Over the centuries – or even millennia – these wandering tribes traversed the whole American continent, from north to south in their search for game. Many millennia before the modern era, they reached Mesoamerica, the Amazon basin and the Andean range as far south as Tierra del Fuego.

In the meantime, around 10 000 B.C., the link between the Asian and American continents was broken as a result of warming of the climate: the level of the oceans rose again and the natural bridge was once again submerged. Consequently, tribes of hunters, armed with stone implements only, left the Old World before the Neolithic revolution had taken place. The point is significant, since among the products of the Neolithic revolution were animal domestication, the beginnings of sedentarnation and agriculture and important technical advances such as weaving, pottery and, later, writing and metal-working.

The Amerindians therefore had to develop independently. They established their own cultural identity without outside influence. Entirely from their own resources, they created a splendid civilization the equal of the other great agricultural civilizations. This point can hardly be overstressed; the civilization of the pre-Columbian peoples is unique.

Lacunae and Cultural Progress

The specificity of the progress accomplished by the pre-Columbian peoples in their evolution towards Neolithic technologies helps to explain the differences both between the Old and New Worlds. It also explains the lacunae in the native cultures of America and the surprisingly advanced techniques characteristic of certain of their civilizations.

The plants on which the agriculture of the Amerindian tribes are based have no connection with those of the Old World: in pre-Columbian society, we find neither the staples of Western food – corn, rye and oats – nor the rice on which Asia based its entire lifestyle. In America, the cultivation of maize emerged at a very early date (its presence dates from around 5000 B.C. in the Andean region and around 3000 B.C. in Mexico). Maize, together with black beans, tomatoes, squashes and pimentoes, formed the basic diet of the Maya and other Mesoamerican peoples. Many varieties of fruit completed their daily fare: papayas, avocados, guavas, cocoa beans, and later pineapples. At an early date, tobacco was cultivated. Agriculture also provided cotton and *maguey* cactus fibre. The husk of the *amate* tree enabled the Maya to manufacture a type of paper for their codices. Finally, the tropical forest provided a host of medicinal plants skilfully employed by the Pre-Columbians.

On the other hand, domesticated animals such as goats, sheep, horses and cattle were unknown to the American, who had no herds of livestock. Apart from dogs, turkeys and bees, and occasionally ducks, there was no animal husbandry in Mesoamerica (unlike the Andean plateaus where lamas, alpacas and guinea pigs were reared).

Similar cultural differences are encountered at the technological level: the pre-Columbians did not possess the plough (their farming tools were limited to the plain digging stick). They did not have the wheel (which appears only in a very few "Mexican" toys), or the potter's wheel (coil-built pots or moulded ceramics were the only kinds known).

Such lacunae prove that there was no communication between the peoples on either side of the Pacific. They show that America developed like an island, with the sole exception of occasional, random contacts, until the 1492 encounter and the Spanish invasion on *terra firma* in the sixteenth century. Between the end of the Paleolithic era and the destruction of the Aztecs at the hands of Cortés, there was no communication between the Old and the New World: neither food crops nor domestic animals were imported into America, and there were neither technological influences, nor religious or cultural exchanges. A few Viking ships may have ventured as far as New England around A.D. 1000. But there is no evidence that their raids had any lasting effect.

In other areas, the pre-Columbians were far from backward. Certain peoples of the New World not only possessed an original form of writing, conveyed in complex glyphs, but were also highly advanced in the field of mathematics and the calendar. Indeed, from the beginning of the modern era, the Maya used a system of numerical notation based on the existence of a "zero" and a positional vigesimal system (based on the number "twenty").

These intellectual tools found application in the computation and measurement of time, where the complexity of the cycles and the methods of establishing dates demanded recourse to numbers so large that the Greeks and Romans would have had great difficulty in formulating them, given the methods at their disposal. This measurement of time, based on a visible astronomy that refined its observations by the aid of endlessly repeated calculations, resorted to true mathematical averages

Surrounded by the virgin forest
The Temple of the Sun of Palenque, dated 690, emerges from the midst of the tropical vegetation. On four tiers, scaled by a central flight of stairs, the temple rises from a base, its façades supported by pillars and its mansard-style roof surmounted by a high *cresteria* (decorative roofcomb), typical of Classic Mayan architecture.

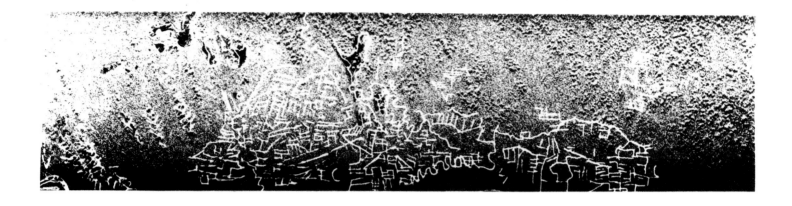

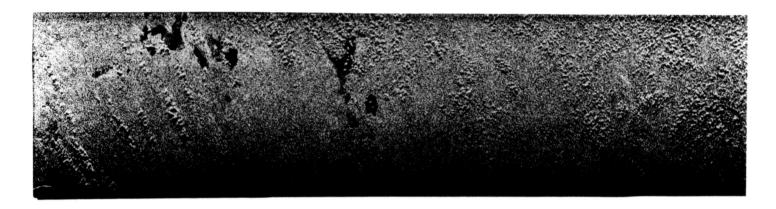

stretching over centuries. By applying a statistical method of calculation, the Maya priests achieved results of amazing precision – to within minutes or even seconds – when measuring astral cycles. Such achievements – in a civilization lacking clocks and time-measuring devices – can not but excite our admiration.

Setting and Environment

The Maya region stretches approximately 1000 km from north to south and 600 km from east to west. It is made up, on the one hand, of lowlands stretching from the Petén region to Tabasco and from Belize to Yucatán, and on the other, of mountainous regions dominated by active volcanoes in South Guatemala, El Salvador and along the western border of Honduras. The entire region lies south of the Tropic of Cancer. The centre is covered by a great Amazonian rainforest, through which runs the Río Usumacinta, a powerful river whose course follows the Mexico-Guatemala frontier. Its muddy waters join those of the Río Grijalva before flowing into the Gulf of Mexico on the Tabasco coast.

Such a hot and humid environment seems little suited to the flourishing of an advanced civilization. The Maya of the Preclassic period therefore had to adapt the terrain in which they established their primitive agriculture. This was a formidable undertaking. In sodden river basins, they established a dense drainage network. These man-made canals, arranged in a geometrical layout, transformed the marshy terrain into land that could be cultivated. The development of such land-use systems is evidence of a prodigious collective effort. It could never have been achieved without the hierarchical social structures and political organisation whose origins date from before the Middle Preclassic period (900–300 B.C.).

Moreover, the lands settled by the Maya were poor in terms of mineral wealth: apart from seams of obsidian near volcanoes and rare outcrops of jade, there were no metals of a kind to permit the development of gold or metal working. Neither gold nor silver occurred naturally on the spot. Copper and bronze technology emerged from other pre-Columbian populations, in places such as Colombia and

A canal network discovered by radar
A veritable drainage network was created by the Maya in the Petén plain: (above) marked in white, one can see the network of canals dug in the Guatemalan virgin forest. Only a special NASA technical process has made it possible to see these works under the thick blanket of vegetation covering the land (below).

The Mayan world
A map of the region where, between the dawn of the modern era and the tenth century A.D., the brilliant civilization of the Maya developed. Lying to the south-east of Mexico, the area includes Guatemala, Belize, the western edge of El Salvador and Honduras, and the Yucatán peninsula, including the states of Chiapas, Campeche, Yucatán and Quintana Roo.

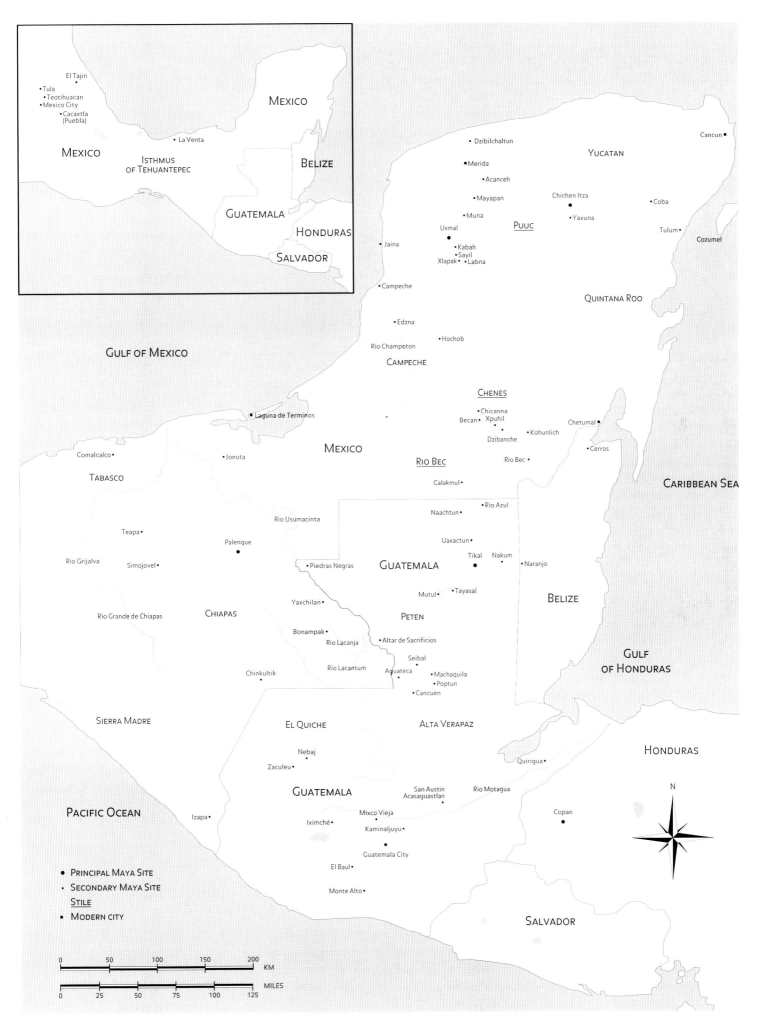

MEXICO

El Tajin
•Tula
•Teotihuacan
•Mexico City
•Cacaxtla
(Puebla)

MEXICO

ISTHMUS
OF TEHUANTEPEC

•La Venta

BELIZE

GUATEMALA

HONDURAS

SALVADOR

•Dzibilchaltun

YUCATAN

Cancun ■

■Merida

•Acanceh

•Mayapan   Chichen Itza •   •Coba

•Muna   PUUC   •Yaxuna

Uxmal ■   Tulum •

•Jaina   •Kabah   Cozumel ■
         •Sayil
Xlapak• •Labna

•Campeche

QUINTANA ROO

•Edzna

         •Hochob
Rio Champoton

CAMPECHE

CHENES

•Chicanna
Becan • •Xpuhil   Chetumal ■
       •Dzibanche   •Kohunlich

GULF OF MEXICO   •Cerros

Laguna de Terminos ■

Comalcalco•   •Jonuta   MEXICO   RIO BEC   Rio Bec •

TABASCO   Calakmul •

                                                   •Rio Azul
                              Rio Usumacinta   Naachtun •

Teapa •   Uaxactun •

        Palenque •   Tikal ● Nakum •

Rio Grijalva   •Piedras Negras   GUATEMALA   •Naranjo
         Simojovel •
                                     Mutul • •Tayasal   BELIZE

Rio Grande de Chiapas   CHIAPAS   Yaxchilan •

                                          PETEN   GULF
                         Bonampak •   OF HONDURAS
                         Rio Lacanja •Altar de Sacrificios

Chinkultik •   Rio Lacantum   Seibal •
                              Aguateca • •Machaquila
                                         •Poptun
                                  •Cancuen

SIERRA MADRE   EL QUICHE   ALTA VERAPAZ   HONDURAS

                     Nebaj •   Quirigua •
         Zaculeu •

CARIBBEAN SEA

PACIFIC OCEAN   San Austin
                                  Acasaguastlan •   Rio Motagua   Copan ●
                     Izapa •   GUATEMALA
                         Iximché • Mixco Vieja
                                •Kaminaljuyu

                              •Guatemala City

• PRINCIPAL MAYA SITE   El Baul •
• SECONDARY MAYA SITE
  STILE   Monte Alto •
■ MODERN CITY
                                                      SALVADOR

N

KM
0   50   100   150   200

MILES
0   25   50   75   100   125

Equador. Trading rafts from these regions supplied the Maya of the late Classic period with their first golden devotional objects, their first golden jewellery and first metal tools.

The Flowering of Architecture

Thanks to their huge land-improvement projects in the flooded terrain of the tropical lowlands, the Maya produced food surpluses which created a labour pool of thousands of workers to build the colossal architectural creations of the late Preclassic period (300 B.C.–A.D. 300) and, more especially, of the Classic period (A.D. 300–900). This mainly involved large urban centres such as Tikal, Uaxactún, Río Azul, Copán, Quiriguá, Palenque, Piedras Negras and Yaxchilán, where grandiose construction schemes were developed.

In the wetlands of Quintana Roo and of Campeche, a different architectural style developed, that of the "Río Bec" and "Chenes" styles. They form the link between the Maya art of Guatemala and the Yucatec style, in sites such as Kohunlich, Becan, Xpuhil, Dzibanché and Chicanná, many of which have only recently been rediscovered.

The vegetation of the Yucatán peninsula – a low, flat, table-like karstic area projecting into the Caribbean sea – becomes sparser the further north one goes. In the northern zone of Yucatán, the tropical forest changes into dense, relatively dry, scrubland on a limestone base where water exists only in underground systems. Vast natural sink-holes, forming wells created by the collapse of the surrounding land – known as *cenotes* – reveal the water table lying below. The inhabitants of the settlements that grew up around these important focal points drew up the water required for their daily existence.

Overlooking the Caribbean Sea
The Mayan city of Tulum, on the eastern coast of Yucatán, dates from the final blossoming of Mayan civilization. With its temples and pyramids facing the sea, it seemed impregnable to the conquistador Juan de Grijalva in 1518 and he did not dare land there.

The architecture that flourished in the north of Yucatán has left admirable works. They are in the "Puuc" style which, in formal and decorative terms, represents the peak of Mayan architecture. Both for purity of layout and technological rigour, Yucatán contains veritable masterpieces: the sites of Uxmal, Kabah, Sayil and Labna feature buildings whose dazzling façades date from the late Classic period (A.D. 800–900).

The Postclassic period (A.D. 900–1200), the final period of development, during which the declining Maya civilization absorbed "Mexican" influences, bears the imprint of the civilizations then dominant in the high plateaus. This resulted in grandiose monuments whose style is a fascinating combination of local art and general Mesoamerican influences. They date the eve of the imperialist era of the Tenochtitlan Aztecs. The focal point of this style is Chichén Itzá, as well as late sites such as Tulum, on the shore of the Caribbean sea.

In Mayan architecture, we encounter one of the greatest expressions of the art conceived by the pre-Columbians for their gods and their sovereigns. The meaning and development of these achievements merit investigation, as do the laws governing them and the intentions of the architects who designed them. The Mayan heritage is our key to a better understanding of the principal civilization of the Mesoamerican world.

Interpreting the Inscriptions

Our understanding of these architectural masterpieces has recently been enhanced thanks to the considerable advances achieved in the decipherment of Maya hieroglyphs. A reading of the texts carved on buildings – on stelae, lintels, bas-reliefs and stairways – has become possible thanks to the combined efforts of eminent specialists who have collaborated for around twenty years to find a solution to this enigmatic code.

Early in the twentieth century, scholars managed to decipher dates, the names

The resplendent façade of the Palace of Uxmal
Almost 100 m long, the frieze composed of stone mosaic on the Palace of the Governor at Uxmal decorates a symmetrical structure standing on an artificial substructure. The confidence of this proud architecture expresses the mastery of the Mayan builders in the ninth and tenth centuries.

of days, months and "centuries" (the latter provided by Fra Diego de Landa in the sixteenth century), and the calculations of the astronomical codices. In particular, specialists unravelled the numerical system expressed by means of bars and dots – a feature, incidentally, that the Maya shared with many other earlier and contemporary cultures, such as the Olmecs of the Gulf coast, the inhabitants of Real Alto, on the Pacific coast, those of Kaminaljuyu, near Guatemala City, the Zapotecs of Oaxaca, and the tribes of La Mojarra, in Veracruz.

But apart from this chronological data, the inscriptions obstinately refused to resign their secrets. Fortunately, the hunches and hard work of researchers such as the Russian linguist Yuri Knorosov, Tatiana Proskuriakov, Heinrich Berlin, and lastly Linda Schele and David Stuart, have helped us not only to understand the meaning of certain signs (the Emblem Glyphs representing cities and the symbols concerning birth, accession to the throne, and marriage), but also to recreate the pronunciation of the syllabic signs peculiar to various Maya dialects. Recently we have been able to read the names of the sovereigns, and reconstruct the life of senior dignitaries and the historical events of the principal dynasties. The essential stages in the lives led by the personalities who ruled the Maya cities during the Classic era have thus become accessible.

This decipherment therefore marks a true revolution in the interpretation of the Maya past. Where we naively imagined a peaceable people, immersed in the contemplation of systems founded on a cyclical measurement of time, and all but obsessed with the implication of the religious calendar, we discover intensely human individuals who were born, married, acceded to the throne, fought wars, sought to dominate their neighbours, took opposing sides in ball-game matches, sacrificed the defeated in bloody rituals, and last but not least ensured that they were accompanied in death by their spouses and slaves, in much the same way as the potentates of Mesopotamia and China.

Rising up from the featureless Yucatán plain
The Temple of Warriors, at Chichén Itzá, preceded by the Portico of the Thousand Columns, is the most characteristic creation of Toltec-Mayan civilization of the eleventh and twelfth centuries, at a time when the city of Tula, on the northern Mexican plateaux, exerted its influence on the northern region of the Mayan territory.

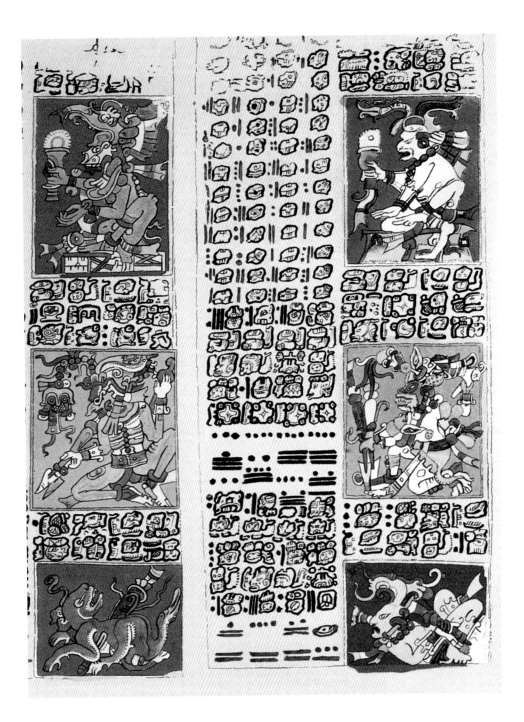

In short, the Maya make a striking entry onto the stage of history. And whereas the monuments of the Preclassic period were in the image of a cosmos whose movement and cycles they symbolized, we discover that the sanctuaries of the Classic period assumed a new meaning: by dedicating them to tutelary deities, the rulers exalted their own power. Pyramids then played the role of ceremonial mausoleums or monuments to a dazzling reign. Buildings were an affirmation of the power and authority of a dynasty aspiring to supremacy. They mark the appearance of an imperialist tendency that found expression in merciless struggle between neighbours – a situation similar to that prevailing among the Greek city states during the Hellenic period.

Thus, stripped of their reputation as a pacific and contemplative people, the Maya have come to resemble many other peoples of history: fighters keen to vanquish their foes – warriors ready to sacrifice their enemies and crush all resistance. Cities clashed, formed alliances, and by turn rose to the rank of metropolises. Art existed in the service not only of the collective power but also, to a greater degree, of personal power: it exalted the glory and the influence of the man who commis-

1   2   3   4   5

A   B

C   D

E   F

G   H

Historical Mayan glyphs

The upper range reproduces historical Mayan signs designating:

1. Date of birth
2. Accession to the throne
3. The emblem of a person named "Shield-Jaguar"
4. The emblem of a person named "Bird-Jaguar"
5. The emblem prefixed to the names and titles of women

(according to M. Coe)

The two columns of glyphs represented on the left denote the names of the most important Mayan cities:

A. Tikal
B. Naranjo
C. Yaxchilán
D. Piedras Negras
E. Palenque
F. Seibal
G. Copán
H. Quiriguá

(according to M. Coe)

sioned it. Adulation of the gods was achieved through worship of the sovereign, who soon assumed the characteristics of divinity.

Aesthetic Forms of Expression

We have already stressed that chance events of prehistory obliged the pre-Columbians to devise their own cultural resources and forms of expression. In architecture, too, they evolved their own language. This was the case both for fundamental laws such as symmetry, rectangularity and axiality (which stem naturally from structures peculiar to vertebrates, to the body and to the human face) and for features of construction such as openings, doors, pillars, columns, capitals, friezes, cornices, staircases, lintels, vaults, and roofs.

There was nothing inevitable about this. Maltese megalithic sanctuaries, for example, with their oval chambers, their apertures hewn out of standing slabs, and their organic layout respecting neither rectangularity nor the horizontal/vertical contrast, are not based on the sacrosanct right angle of the builders of Antiquity. Maya architects could have adopted a similarly unusual and baffling approach. Yet they developed a constructive system that presents certain similarities with the civilizations of Antiquity.

The similarities between Maya architecture and that of the Ancient World is so evident that the first discoverers of the cities buried in the virgin rainforest of Mexico and the Petén even supposed that the Amerindians had been influenced by Egypt, Babylon and Classical Antiquity. In the middle of this century, similarities with the monuments of Angkor – with their corbelled vaults, sanctuaries supported by high pyramids covered in flights of steps, and stone balusters – once again raised the issue of trans-Pacific contacts.

Indeed the slight convexity of the columns of the palaces of Yucatán call to mind the form of Greek columns, and the carved reliefs containing ritual scenes evoke Pharaonic art. Mayan representation of the human figure had given rise to the same speculations: were not the dignitaries depicted on the bas-reliefs of Palenque related, by certain distortions, to those of the tombs of Memphis and Thebes? Their faces and legs seen in profile, shoulders often face on, hieratic gestures, an absence of perspective abolishing all notion of space, and an association with hieroglyphic inscriptions, all contributed to this conclusion.

While they knew neither the wheel nor the potter's wheel, the pre-Columbians nevertheless reinvented the great laws of composition underpinning town-planning and architecture: they knew how to handle the volumes and arenas of architectural space, they surrounded buildings with flat esplanades and they alternated the horizontal masses of palaces and the vertical accents of pyramids. They constructed terraces and esplanades in order to create different levels for building, they composed complexes punctuated by relief sculpture and built veritable triumphal arches. In short, they used their monuments to convey the outward signs of power and civilization.

This is why the study of Maya architecture constitutes one of the best tools for understanding the extraordinary civilization of this pre-Columbian people, who lived in a luxuriant tropical setting and engaged in a long struggle against a natural environment often hostile to man. Their triumph was to make this inhospitable environment the scene of a flourishing culture.

THE ARCHITECTURAL LANGUAGE
OF THE MAYA

Laws and Techniques of the Builders

Page 19
The Mayan ball game
This stone disk, 55 cm in diameter, which served as a marker on a ball court in Chinkultik (Chiapas), dates from A.D. 590. It shows a kneeling ball player, wearing a padded belt and ceremonial head-dress. In front of him is depicted the huge ball of solid gum over which the rival teams fought during in this sacred Pre-Columbian "sport". (Mexico City, National Museum of Anthropology)

Mayan "portrait"
This expressive small terracotta head (8.5 cm high), dating from the latter part of the Classic period (seventh to eighth centuries), represents a Mayan with the usual ornamental extension of the bridge of the nose protruding from the forehead. The mouth, open in a fixed grin, reveals the teeth, whereas the large, strongly delineated eyes show a certain "expressionism". (Barcelona, Barbier-Mueller Museum)

In the context of pre-Columbian architecture, the œuvre of the Maya occupies a special position. Representatives of one of the main strands of Mesoamerican civilizations, the Maya created distinctive buildings that stand apart from the accomplishments of all the other peoples of the New World.

The difference lay in the fact that the buildings erected in Maya territory included a solid roof – the corbelled or stepped vault – achieved by means of a mortar mixed with rubble forming a quasi-monolithic concrete. This means not only that their monuments have shown a greater resistance to the ravages of time, man and nature, but also that, even today, the interiors remain relatively intact. Consequently, the historian can comprehend the objectives and preoccupations of their creators.

Architecture is an essential source of information about the pre-Columbian peoples. It allows one to visualize the existence of the tribes who lived in the great forests of the Petén and the Usumacinta basin. In addition, it encompasses sculpture, painting, inscriptions, town-planning concepts and the physical expression of religion and power. Around this architecture, the great undertakings of a whole nation were concentrated. It unlocks the door to an entire civilization which might otherwise have remained inaccessible.

We should therefore situate this art in the context of pre-Columbian thinking and, more specifically, of Maya thinking. Above all, we must not lose sight of the following fact: superficial study might lead one to imagine a link between Maya architecture and the great creations of the West or of Asia (Egypt, Mesopotamia, Greece, or Angkor). But no such link exists. These similarities do not stem from a common heritage that the Amerindians shared with the populations of the Ancient World: as previously stated, the cultural inheritance of the pre-Columbian peoples is entirely the creation of tribes who ventured into America via Alaska even before the Neolithic era. The hunter-gatherers who populated central America had no memories of architecture from their homeland, where it appeared only at a much later date. They had no tradition and no building technology. They began from scratch.

From Hut to Pyramid

In Maya architecture, all structures derive from the ancestral hut, with wattle-and-daub walls covered with a roof made of palms over a wooden frame. The vernacular dwelling – perfectly adapted to the tropical climate – consisted, for each household, of one or two huts often placed parallel to one another. Each hut contained a single interior space, lit by a square doorway built into one of the long sides of the building. There was sometimes a second doorway to provide better air circulation.

The floor plan was rectangular or oval, in which case the shorter sides of the hut were rounded, giving a conical form to the ends of the roof. This traditional style of hut – still visible today in the villages of Yucatán – is a survival of the time-honoured vernacular dwelling of the pre-Columbian period. It has changed little since the dawn of Maya society, 3 000 years ago.

The significance of this construction in perishable materials lies in the fact that, for the Maya, it constituted the archetype of all their architectural schemes. As such, it exerted a considerable influence on stone architecture, as much as by its exterior forms (with sloping roofs), as by its interior space. The study of ancient Maya buildings shows that the permanent constructions were, essentially, a transposition into stone – a "petrification" – of the primitive hut. It was the hut that inspired the interior arrangement of the palaces and sanctuaries built at the top of the pyramids. It is the open- and lath-work of the hut that recurs on the façade of the great stone buildings. The use of ties made of rope or of jungle creeper wrapped round the straw padding of the hut walls inspired the outline and rhythms of the great ornamental friezes of the stone buildings. It inspired the square door, with wooden lintel, that stands unmodified at the entrance of palace and temple "chambers".

The stone buildings rise up on ever higher platforms. In much the same way, the humble Maya family built a small earth platform as foundation in order to keep its dwelling beyond the reach of floods, which were frequent during the rainy season. These platforms increased as other elements were added to them. The enlargement

"Anatomy" of a Mayan vault
The ruined façade of this building in Copán reveals the technique of the corbelled vault characteristic of Mayan architecture: its stone blocks projecting out over each other, embedded in mortar stonework, make it possible to cover a narrow chamber with surfaces of meticulously dressed stone.

The common dwelling

For thousands of years, the Mayan hut, with its wattle-and-daub walls and thatched roofs, constituted the traditional dwelling of the people of Yucatán. A single door in the centre of the longer side gave access to the interior.

Page 22 right
The technique of permanent coffering

In the Yucatán style known as "Puuc", the formula of the Mayan vault evolved: now the stone blocks forming the visible surface of the building served as coffering into which concrete was poured. Regular flat surfaces resulted from this technique, as well as a lightening of the structure: the spar of the vaults increased and the builders supported them on a portico formed of low pillars.

of basements (substructures) in the form of platforms reached colossal dimensions during the Classic period. But whatever their proportions, they owed their origins to the little mound of earth on which the hut was built.

When the earliest tribes – in the formative period between 2 000 and 1 000 B.C. – built the first religious centres dedicated to their cosmic divinities, they conceived the abode of their gods in the image of the hut: walls of wattle-and-daub and roof of palm leaves. But these first sanctuaries stood apart from ordinary dwellings because of the height of the platforms on which they stood. Terraces made of materials accumulated over centuries formed the base of the temples. In enlarging and raising them, the Maya constructed powerful pyramidal pedestals to support the house of the deity.

The tradition of adding new platforms on top of old ones in order to place the ritual *cella* ever higher had two consequences. It obliged the builders to incorporate a central staircase linking the ground to the level of the sanctuary at the front of the edifice; it also laid the foundations of a fundamental principle of pre-Columbian architecture – the law of superposed structures.

This principle – which meant that religious centres were always rebuilt on the same site, and that a new, larger construction was always built on top of the old pyramid – is a constant one; it probably explains the huge scale of the Maya pyramids, some of which attain 70 m in height. This was a system of architectural development peculiar to the pre-Columbians. It means that archaeologists working on a ruined building can be confident that its structure buries and protects an earlier building, which is often better preserved.

Above
The Mayan house
Inside the hut, decorated with carefully lime-washed mud-walls, one can see the fine internal structure of the roof, made of plaited palms. This basic structure was copied in stone in the rooms and chambers of the palaces where the Mayan elite lived during the Classic period. Weaving and the production of hammocks – common to the Tainos of the Caribbean and which appeared among the Maya only after the Conquest – occupy the present inhabitants.

Below left
A simple structure
In Yucatán, the Mayan hut often possesses oval walls beneath the thatched roof. The whitewashed mud covering, which cannot withstand the violent seasonal downpours, often has to be renewed.

Below right
The dwelling unit
Elevation and plan of the traditional Mayan hut.

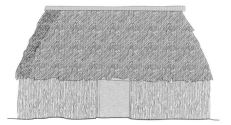

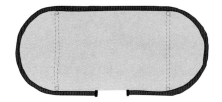

Depiction of the hut
On one of the friezes of the Nunnery Quadrangle at Uxmal, a depiction of the traditional Mayan hut – topped here by an emblematic serpent with two heads – figures above the doors leading into the rooms of a palace.

The hut turned to stone
The image of the Mayan house is often represented on palace friezes. The motif represented here on a façade underlines the relationship between the original rustic model and its transposition into stone.

The Composition of the Palaces

The stone architecture of the Maya is made up of two major classes of buildings. The first of these, as just mentioned, are the pyramids. Often the result of successive superpositions, they constitute a sort of hymn in stone dedicated to the gods. Only the clergy were allowed to scale their vast stairways stretching up to the heavens. The second are a series of vast buildings conceived on a horizontal plan, which are described as palaces.

This contrast between vertical and horizontal structures reflects, as we shall see, the contrast between the abode of the gods and the homes of mere mortals, though the inhabitants of the palaces formed a small elite. For only those who held power (kings, priests, warriors, and scholars) occupied stone buildings; the populace continued, for the most part, to live in traditional huts.

What differentiated the interior spaces of the "tower" and the horizontal blocks? It has to be said that nothing distinguishes the *cella* of a pyramid from the chamber of a palace. In both cases, we see the same "petrification" of the humble hut: the same restricted dimensions that derive from the proportions of a single living room, the same stone roofing created by means of a corbelled vault imitating the internal space of the thatched hut. In short, concrete architecture reproduces the same forms, in both temple and palace.

The only difference lies in the disposition of the rooms: at the top of the pyramid, the transversal *cella* stood alone, or was duplicated by the creation of a second identical space behind the first chamber, communicating through a doorway. In certain cases, such as the great temples of Tikal, there was even a third dark, mysterious ritual chamber. Here, three rectangular spaces were therefore placed one behind the other.

A radiant style of architecture
The façade of the western building of the Nunnery Quadrangle at Uxmal exemplifies the style of these palaces of Yucatán, where high-ranking dignitaries, priests and sovereigns lived. Contrasting with the simple, geometric forms, the burgeoning decoration combines various Mayan religious symbols.

Page 27
The rebirth of Tikal
Emerging from the tropical forest that had overrun them, the buildings of the great Mayan capital of Guatemala have been the focus of intensive restoration work. Here, Temple I of Tikal displays its steep staircase leading to the high sanctuary, crowned with a *cresteria* at a total height of 45 m.

The palaces, on the other hand, contained a whole series of chambers set side by side, without lateral communication. Chambers opened onto the façade through square doors, behind the first row, there was a second series of rooms. These latter were darker as they received daylight only via the first room.

This formula led the Maya to design very long buildings containing a large number of rooms distributed according to diverse geometrical schemes. The imagination demonstrated by Maya architects is illustrated by the infinite variety of ground plans of these palaces. The largest ones reached a length of 100 m, with a total of twenty or thirty rooms distributed in ten or fifteen independent "apartments". The complex sometimes contained a much larger central hall, which was presumably intended for public meetings or required by court ritual.

The architectural profile of these dwelling units varied greatly: a simple low structure block built on a platform; two or more low storeys with the upper storeys recessed; or a combination of four low rectangular blocks forming a quadrangle with a vast courtyard or central patio. Horizontal palaces and vertical pyramids thus constituted the fundamental components of Mayan urban design.

The Ball Game – a Mesoamerican Ritual

Beside the pyramids and the palaces, one of the architectural features characteristic of the Mesoamerican urban centre was the ball court. A ball game was practised by almost all the pre-Columbian peoples in the regions stretching from the Petén forest up to the upland Mexican plateaus. Its existence is already documented at the time of the Olmecs at La Venta in around 1000 B.C. As a competitive match played between two teams, the ball game had complex rules. It was played with a large ball of solid gum weighing some one to three kilos. The players had to propel the ball with the trunks of their bodies, without using their arms or legs. Their bodies were protected by a broad, thick belt of fabric, wood and cotton padding. The object was to score "goals" represented by poles or by rings fixed in the side walls of the ball court. The game sometimes finished with the vanquished party being put to death, in a ritual that was based on the calendar and on astral cycles.

In architectural terms, the ball court was an open space, closed in on the sides by two parallel banks, sloping inwards to a greater or lesser degree, and by walls surrounding the actual "pitch". A wider area at each end, intended for the teams, gave the whole area a plan in the form of a flattened letter H.

In the town-planning of Maya cities, the ball game represented an important element that went beyond the purely recreational; it had a religious function and was part of the sacrificial ritual. The importance of this complex should not be underestimated. It was central to the Maya society and way of life.

There were, of course, other types of Maya buildings: observatories, steam baths, and sacrificial altars, which completed the city plan. In addition, though they had neither horse-drawn transport – they did not possess the wheel – riding animals nor beasts of burden, the Maya constructed vast straight causeways from one town to another: the *sacbeob* (plural of *sacbé*) or "white roads". These could extend over many kilometres and seem to have been intended for both religious ceremonies and court processions. These processional routes were built and levelled with the aid of heavy stone rollers hauled by teams of workers.

Building Techniques

Neither wood nor stone was scarce in the area occupied by the Maya. The extensive rainforest provided mahogany and the timber of the *zapote* or sapodilla, used for door lintels and the sculpted decorations that covered the interiors of the temples built at the top of the pyramids.

The karstic structure of the Yucatán peninsula provided good quality limestone, which was variously white, pink or grey and ideally suited to being dressed and

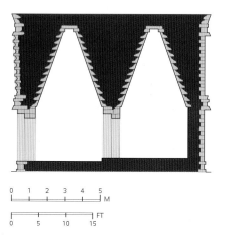

Palace construction
This section of a Puuc-style building in Yucatán shows the technique adopted for the construction of public or private chambers – usually placed one behind the other – in Mayan palaces. The rubble stonework (shown in dark shading) is poured in cement form into a permanent casing, whose blocks are held in place by projecting pins, while the visible outer surface, on the outside as on the inside, is smooth and meticulously joined.

The "national sport" of the Maya
The ball court in the centre of the city of Copán (Honduras) displays its lateral banks overlooked by the ceremonial buildings. Here, teams competed, using the heavy "pelota" of gum. As in the Olympic Games in ancient Greece, these Mayan tournaments had a religious component.

carved. In the mountainous volcanic regions, trachyte, basalt and tufa were used to build walls of small regular stonework.

But before the construction of any building could begin, its basement had to be created. It has already been indicated that these "podia" could attach proportions. Some platforms reached a total length of 150 to 200 m, a width of 100 to 150 m, and a height of 8 to 10 m, representing a volume of 200 000 to 250 000 m². This mass of materials weighs around half a million tons. And it represents just one platform of one building constructed on level land at Uxmal.

What is more, the Maya displaced much greater volumes than this in order to create terraces and acropolises. This is the case, in particular, at Copán. In order to complete the massive terracing works, hundreds, or even thousands, of workers were necessary. Men carried the building materials on their backs in organised teams requisitioned during the dry season, when agriculture did not require much manpower. Even when raw materials existed on site, the construction sites demanded major infrastructure work, as much for the supply of food as for the organisation of the work.

As for the stone structure itself, the challenge was more complex. Initially, Maya masons built walls of dressed stone and corbelled stonework vaults. Then, once they had perfected the technique of making concrete, roofing was created with "monolithic" structures of concrete, poured inside a facing made of carefully dressed stone which formed permanent coffering. The genius of the Maya was, indeed, to conceive a system whereby the outer blocks of stone, carefully joined together without mortar, were capable of containing the liquid cement mixed with rubble making wooden coffering unnecessary. The outer stone casing was built gradually, with the cement poured in at intervals so that, as the wall rose, the cement was able to harden in a succession of superposed layers.

In order to make Maya concrete, high-quality mortar was indispensable. In the Yucatec region, where limestone was freely available, this technique was highly sophisticated. The lime mortar was obtained by placing crushed stone on a pile of dry wood which was then set alight; the brasier "fired" the stones. The amount of quicklime produced by this method was small, whereas the amount of wood consumed was huge. The almost total disappearance of the primitive Yucatec forest, progressively replaced by dense, inpenetrable scrub, can be attributed to this highly wasteful method of working – at a time when the kiln was unknown.

We should also describe how the monoliths for sculpted stelae were transported. These blocks reached impressive dimensions and weighed many tons: for example, a stela at Quiriguá measures over 10.6 m in height and weighs 65 tons. Such blocks of stone were moved, as in the Egypt of the Pharaohs, by teams of workers using ropes and rollers or sledges dragged along a path of clay.

Decoration of Maya Monuments

In the Maya conception of architecture, one cannot dissociate structures from their decorative component. This is obvious in relation to concrete work, where the outer surface – which often includes raised ornamentation – is an integral part of the construction. As we shall show, this technique entailed a standardized production of hundreds of similar blocks to make up the "components" of repetitive motifs, particularly in the "Puuc" style: masks, open-work slabs, and so on. This required a veritable mass production well ahead of its time and is one of the most original technological features of Maya art.

In the early period, however, the ornamental elements, arranged on the sloping sides of the pyramids, were created by means of highly contoured stucco motifs. This is the case for the enormous masks of deities that cover the stepped base of a series of buildings dating from the Preclassic period. In particular, a pyramid at Uaxactún (Structure H-Sub 3) in the Petén, the first temple of Cerros (Structure 5C-2) in Belize, or the Pyramid of the Masks at Kohunlich in Quintana Roo illustrate this point. The sculpted plaster – with its rich painted polychrome finish, partially

Building in the image of the gods
In the centre of Mayan territory, certain pyramids are decorated with large stucco reliefs of deities or sovereigns: thus, at Kohunlich, in the Río Bec region, the excavated façade of the main temple comprises three decorated levels: on either side of a stairway stand high relief masks, which were once brightly painted.

The image of the god Chac repeated ad infinitum
On the façade of the Palace of Masks, or "Codz Poop" of Kabah (Yucatán), the stylized mask of the rain god has an obsessive quality. Its protruding eyes, long, trunk-shaped nose and rigorous frontal symmetry cover the whole building.

erased today – was affixed to a support of stone: projecting blocks formed an "armature" which supported the highly sculpted elements, such as the nose or the headdress of the deity.

In buildings of the "Chenes" style (at Yucatán, Campeche and Quintana Roo), the whole façade represents a huge mask of the cosmic monster. In such cases a mouth boasting a row of huge canines forms the doorway to the sanctuary (Building II at Chicanná, Campeche, or the temple west of the Pyramid of the Magician at Uxmal). This form of decoration transformed a plain wall into sculpture and eliminated the division between architecture and decoration. The building was transformed into the terrifying mouth of a snake, ready to swallow up the visitor. The effect of this symbolic motif, handled in a vigorous geometrical abstraction, is striking. It demonstrates the mastery of the architect as sculptor.

When describing the ornamental elements of the buildings, we should not omit to mention the Codz Poop, or the Palace of Masks at Kabah, whose façade is covered with dozens of effigies of the god Chac stacked one on top of the other. It is characteristic of "Puuc" art to create a recurrent design, achieved by a veritable jigsaw puzzle in stone, with highly stylized elements.

To the east of a palace at Kabah, archaeologists have recently uncovered fine emblematic figures carved in the round. These sculptures originally stood against an east-facing façade, and have been restored to their original position by the archaeologists excavating the site. They are life-size and demonstrate a remarkable sense of sculptural values. Despite a certain rigidity in the sculpting of the body, conveying a robotic quality, this sculpture – similar, in its close association with architecture, to the sculpture on the pediment of Greek temples – is a discovery of considerable importance.

The role of painting in Maya art was also of prime importance. The discovery in 1946 at Bonampak (Chiapas) of a palace whose rooms were covered in painted scenes, dating from 792, confirms a remarkable pictorial sense, which is also found in the finest Maya pottery. The paintings also show the major role that polychromy played in architecture. These frescoes of monumental significance have today, unfortunately, been almost completely effaced by humidity. Only identical copies convey the original impression, preserving the message of this all too ephemeral art. The value of such works lies in the importance attached to the vivid depiction of man. Although portrayed in a stylized manner, the figures convey a sense of movement by their very natural poses.

The skill of the artist is revealed, in particular, in a scene showing prisoners sentenced to sacrifice. By using a layered composition, the painter is able to arrange the figures freely in various poses. In its representational mode, Maya pictorial art demonstrates a fine mastery of figurative solutions. It faithfully reproduces down to the smallest detail the ceremonial costume of the ruler and his "nobles". All these scenes are depicted in brilliant colours in striking contrast with the sober exterior of the buildings as they appear today.

But the natural stone finish they now display conveys a false impression. Maya buildings were generally covered with a layer of quick-lime and then painted. The accounts of the first travellers to visit Palenque and the rare vestiges of pigment remaining on the palaces and pyramids, confirm that rich colours (a vivid red-or-ange) once covered the urban landscape.

An offering to the gods
Masked, wearing a plumed head-dress and sitting cross-legged, this priest shown on the side of a polychrome Mayan vase from the site of Alta Verapaz places his offering in front of the sanctuary of the god. (Guatemala City, Popol Vuh Museum)

A painted palace

A room in the palace of Bonampak (Chiapas), covered in a superb painted scheme, as American explorers by chance discovered it in 1946. This copy presented to the National Museum of Anthropology of Mexico City now replaces the originals that have been almost totally destroyed by humidity in less than fifty years. It bears witness to the extraordinary quality of Mayan wall painting at the end of the eighth century.

Page 32 below
Anthropomorphic wall

The main construction of the Mayan site of Chicanná (Campeche) is decorated with a façade in the Chenes style. The sanctuary is a schematic representation of the god: the doorway depicts two stylized eyes above a huge mouth, edged with powerful fangs, in a representation of the monster Itzamna, creator of the universe.

The enigmatic face of the Maya

This very simple stucco head depicts a reflective person with fleshy lips and eyes that seem absorbed in a dream. The extension into the forehead of the bridge of the nose is part of the "canon" of Mayan beauty. (Oaxaca, Rufino Tamayo Museum)

THE GREAT CLASSIC CITIES

Tikal – a Jungle Metropolis

Page 35

Funerary mask of Río Azul

This extraordinary object, carved in a block of green fuchsite, is enhanced by the addition of shells for the spiral motif of the eyes and for the triangular tongue (characteristic of the god named G 1 by the experts, a deity of the night sun). It is decorated with lightly carved scroll motifs, heightened with traces of vermilion. (Barcelona, Barbier-Mueller Museum)

Ritual of the ball game

Two players, wearing protective outfits (wide belt and padding) on either side of a large "pelota" of gum are depicted on this goal marker from Cancuen (Petén), dating from 795. The confrontations of this sacred "sport" included a bloody ritual: the execution of the losers. (Guatemala City, National Museum of Archaeology and Ethnology)

The emergence of the great Maya cities was a slow process. It began at the end of the Preclassic period, around 200 or 100 B.C. But to understand how the first centres of religions and political power arose, we have to go much further back. The settlements built by the Olmecs of the Gulf of Mexico around 1200–1000 B.C. mark the origins of the pre-Columbian ceremonial centres. These complexes incorporated the two main recurrent features: the pyramid and the ball court.

At La Venta, in the marshy region of Tabasco, the Olmecs built a conical earth pyramid 125 m in diameter and 31.5 m high, totalling some 20 000 tons of earth and rubble. Here, too, the first advanced civilization of ancient Mexico created a monumental sports ground between two parallel banks of earth 80 m long. At the northern extremity of this complex was an area in the form of a rectangle. The three elements – pyramid, ball court and rectangle – are arranged on an accurate north-south axis in the centre of an island in a tributary of the Río Tonala. The complex also includes tumuli and a series of colossal monoliths, in particular altars and stelae, as well as huge stone heads. The latter, admirably sculpted, represent helmet-wearing ball-game players. These works, weighing up to 25 tons mark the birth of great sculptural art in Mexico.

Such is the legacy inherited by the first Maya tribes. It included the rudiments of a system of glyphs permitting the notation of names and the recording of numbers by means of dots (1) and bars (5) that serve to denote the dates of a sacred calendar based on complex astronomical data.

Burgeoning Religious Centres

Situated in an alluvial environment – stone was rare and had to be imported by raft from quarries many kilometres away – the Olmec monuments were built, for the most part, of compressed earth. They were, in effect, artificial halls of allusion. This material came from cleaning the canals, which was necessary to maintain the drainage and irrigation system. In this way, Olmec architecture was built entirely of earth, as for a long time were the first Maya constructions. It consisted of impressive volumes whose accumulation formed platforms and banks, as well as pyramids whose incline could be no steeper than the natural slippage of the Olmec's unitable materials permitted.

The influence of sculptural creations of the Olmecs – in particular the colossal heads – was felt much later as far as the Pacific coast, in the south of present-day Guatemala, at La Democracia and Monte Alto. Stelae also appear at La Venta, but do not yet display the accomplishment shown by the superb later examples, decorated with bas-relief figures, discovered by archaeologists in Kaminaljuyu (300 B.C.–A.D.150) not far from present-day Guatemala City. Finally, in Veracruz, the stela of La Mojarra marks the appearance, in A.D. 156, of a style known as "epi-Olmec" where the effigy of the figure is accompanied by a long inscription in glyphs similar to those used by the Maya.

Olmec monument
This huge monolithic altar from the Olmec site of La Venta, in the Gulf (Tabasco), shows a figure sitting cross-legged, wearing a crown in the image of a jaguar, beneath a relief sculpture in its turn exhibiting a schematic image of the jaguar in its role as earth monster. Emerging from a mythical cave, the figure holds a rope to which a captive sentenced to sacrifice is tied. (Villahermosa, Museum Park of La Venta)

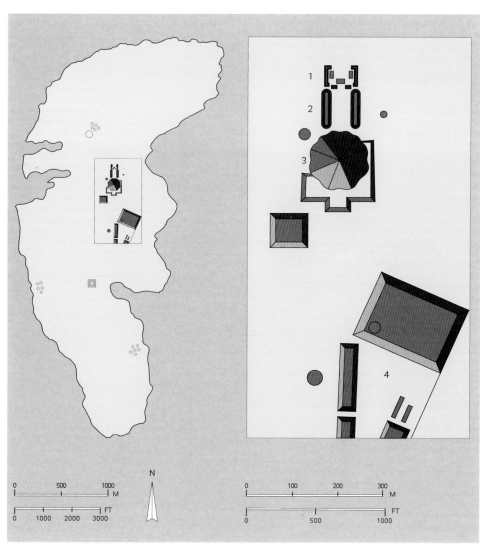

A site 3 000 years old
The island of La Venta, in the marshlands of Río Tonala. On the right, in detail, a plan showing the arrangement of the sacrificial centre on a north/south axis:
1. Quadrangle
2. The two banks of the ball court
3. Earth pyramid
4. Stirling Group

Colossal Olmec effigy
This monolithic sculpture of basalt, 241 cm high and weighing around 25 tons, was sculpted in La Venta between 1000 and 800 B.C. It probably represents – beneath stylized traits – an Olmec king wearing a helmet similar to those worn by ball-game players. (Villa-hermosa, Museum Park of La Venta)

Monte Alto monolithic head
After the fashion of the colossal heads of La Venta – but of smaller proportions – the monoliths discovered at La Democracia and Monte Alto, on the Pacific coast of Guatemala, offer late Preclassic examples inspired by the Olmec formula.

A Pre-Mayan funerary sculpture
In their Guatemalan manifestation – a late transformation of the Olmec style – the colossal heads of La Democracia have changed in appearance: they no longer depict ball-game players with eyes open wide, but people whose abstracted look and closed eyes seem to commemorate a death.

An emblematic stela
On the site of Kaminaljuyu, not far from the present-day capital of Guatemala, emerged the mysterious civilization that, around 100 B.C. created the first stelae sculpted in the Mayan style. This work, 183 cm high, carved in granite, represents a high-ranking dignitary wearing a mask of the "god with the long nose". (Guatemala City, National Museum of Archaeology and Ethnology)

The radiating influence of the Olmec centre is thus discernible in a series of works all exhibiting features that can be traced back to La Venta, Tres Zapotes or San Lorenzo. In Maya territory, architecture soon followed the same evolution – with pyramid and ball court – in the first cities built in the Petén and in the *sierras* of the volcanic regions of Guatemala and Honduras. The buildings – defined as "structures" by archaeologists – belonging to that common tradition are platforms, first in earth, then in stone, which were surmounted by sanctuaries roofed with palm-fronds. Their layout was simple: it consisted of one or two square or rectangular superposed platforms, each level smaller than the one below, ornamented with large decorative stucco masks. A central staircase led to the sanctuary of the summit of which only low walls and the marks of foundation posts remain – vestigial traces of a primitive *cella*.

Left
The goal of the ball game
Also from Kaminaljuyu, this stela
with two openings also dates from
the so-called Miraflores period,
between 300 B.C. and A.D. 150.
Its decoration includes stylized
emblems as yet undeciphered.
(Guatemala City, National
Museum of Archaeology and
Ethnology)

Right
A mysterious Guatemalan stela
This basalt stela from El Baul,
2.96 m high, shows a ball player.
The figure wears a coyote mask
and tramples a beaten opponent
underfoot. Below, a frieze of
six small figures may depict the
victorious team. Hieroglyphics
can be seen above left. This work,
created by the southern neighbours of the Maya, seems to
display Mexican influence
(seventh or eighth century).

Fortunately, examples of such structures have survived to the present day. One example has been discovered at Cerros in Belize, (Structure 5C-2) and dates back to A.D. 50. Similarly, at Uaxactún, near Tikal, the H-Sub 3 pyramid features large superposed stucco masks. Lastly, the pyramid known as E-VII Sub, which was excavated in 1927, shows similar decoration, but this time applied to all four sides of the building, based on a double symmetry, both axial and orthogonal. Here, too, the presence of large stucco masks on two levels depicting stylized wild beasts shows a highly formalized representation of the gods.

This type of religious building, present also at Edzná and at Kohunlich, testifies to the symbolic concerns that found expression in structures built for religious purposes. The research of Linda Schele and David Freidel shows that the building of Cerros had a cosmological meaning connected with the ritual procession of the

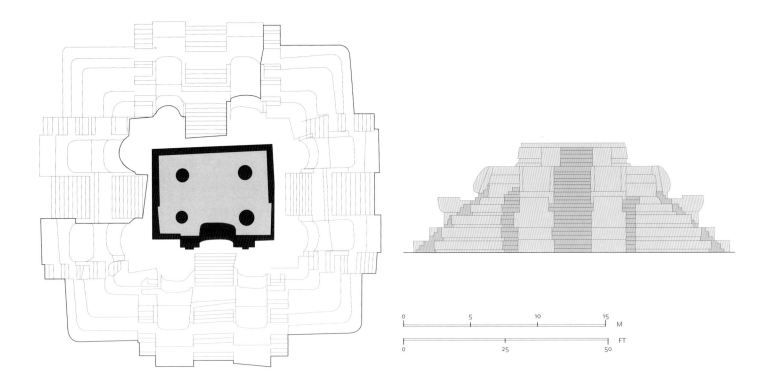

priest-kings. Situated on the lower level of the façade, on either side of the staircase, was the schematic image of the Sun rising on the right and setting on the left. Similarly, on the higher level, the images of the Morning Star on the one hand and the Evening Star on the other depicted the two visible aspects of the planet Venus, which played a primordial role in the correlation between the astronomical calendar of 365 days and the holy calendar of 260 days.

This research clearly demonstrates the close link that exists between architecture and religion through a semiological system that conveyed a rigorous representation of the Universe and the "mechanics" of the heavens. Everywhere in the Maya worlds, religious buildings must be linked to the sacred world inhabited by this people, it was this reality that the architects attempted to express symbolically in their devotional buildings.

The Construction of the Great Pyramids

It was at Tikal that the gigantism of Classic Maya architecture attained its apogee. In this huge metropolis which, at its peak, accommodated tens of thousands of inhabitants and consumed the produce of much of the surrounding Petén region, the concentration of political and religious power led to huge concerted efforts in the building of a complex of grandiose monuments, whose sacred function was linked to a ceremonial role.

It took half a millennium for the concept of the Maya pyramid to reach its largest dimensions: it can be argued that a steady evolution led from the platforms of Cerros (19 x 14 m and 5 m in height, or 1 300 m^3 in volume) and Uaxactún at the dawn of the modern era (25 m^2 and 9 m high, or 5 000 m^3) to the colossal pyramid of Temple IV at Tikal (70 m high on a base of 60 by 50 m approximately, or 75 000 m^3) dating from the seventh century A.D. The volume of the construction forming the substructure of the upper sanctuary multiplied by sixty in one case and by fifteen in the other, but the function changed very little: on the huge base – usually in superposed levels, each recessed one above the other – the *cella,* which was once built of perishable materials, has turned into a double or triple stone chamber topped by a *cresteria* (or high ornamental "roof comb").

In the form of a deity
Mayan incense burner in two sections, created in black terracotta with incised decoration (sixth century) from Uaxactún. It shows the god Q sitting cross-legged. Similar pottery has been found at Kaminaljuyu. (Guatemala City, National Museum of Archaeoloy and Ethnology)

A representation of the universe
A reconstruction of the first temple of Cerros (Belize), with its two platforms covered in polychrome stucco reliefs. Under the name of Building 5C-2, this building dating from A.D. 50 is decorated, on the first level, with motifs representing the sun rising and the sun setting and, on the second level, with the planet Venus in its manifestation as Morning Star and Evening Star. The upper sanctuary probably possessed two "poles" symbolising the cosmic trees (according to Linda Schele).

Page 42 below
Mayan influence
A survey drawing of the stela of La Mojarra (Veracruz), dating from A.D. 156, where the figure rendered in a Mayan style is surrounded by a hieroglyphic inscription in a proto-Zoquean language, similar to that spoken at Kaminaljuyu.

At that time the sanctuary was formed by tiny communicating rooms, covered by a concrete corbelled vault whose shape reproduced the inner space of the traditional hut of cob and thatch. It was here that rituals of a religious and cosmological nature took place. Compared to the solid volume of the pyramid, the hollow space that formed the sanctuary represented less than a l00th, sometimes even a 150th of the cube area of the building.

Whereas the conical surface of the Olmec earth pyramid of La Venta did not exceed an angle of 35°, the gradient at Tikal reached a vertiginous 70°, with a phenomenal flight of stairs whose steps are twice as high as they are wide. The angle of incline of the sides of these extraordinary man-made mountains – they contained some 150 000 tons of stone and rubble – no longer related to the angle at which accumulated building materials would naturally slide. Stonework now took the place of packed earth and the realization represented a remarkable technological feat. Masterful use of mortar was the key to building the pyramid. It includes a carefully dressed outer layer of stone. The smooth finish of the dressed stone is highlighted by the changes of level, whose outlines modulate the massive structure.

The three levels in Temple II have become nine in Temple I. They represent a vigorous structuralization of the pyramidal mass. On each level, the near vertical sides are set off by a groove running round the base. The spirited sculptural treatment of volume and the regular rhythm of these horizontal lines form a striking contrast with the salient staircase that soars upward in one sweep from the base to the topmost platform on which the sanctuary stands, surmounted in its turn by the *cresteria* 8 to 10 m in height.

What it was like to Work on a Maya Building Site
What did a building site in a metropolis like Tikal, surrounded by forest, look like? In order to get some idea, we should remember, on the one hand, that the city boasted several large pyramids, which reached heights of between 45 and 70 m, and, on the other, that vast palace quarters alternated with religious buildings. The

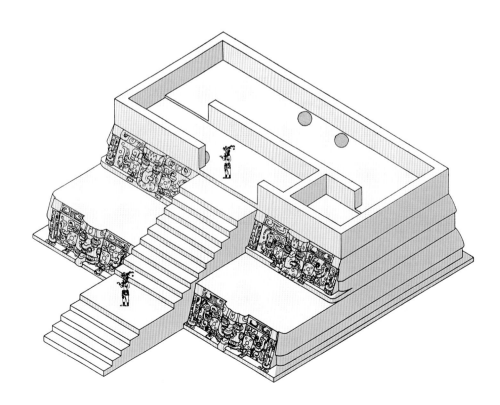

The ceremonial centre of Tikal
This aerial view encompasses the heart of the great Mayan city of Tikal (Petén): in the centre, the main square, surrounded by stelae. To the left stands Temple I, to the right Temple II dominates; in the foreground, the northern acropolis and, in the background on the left, the central acropolis. All these buildings, dating between A.D. 650 and 800, have been cleared and restored since 1956.

A three-storey pyramid
Temple II at Tikal, seen from the
summit of Temple I, with its three
levels scaled by a central stairway
and its *cella* surmounted with a
high decorative *cresteria*. At the
back, Temple III and the huge
Temple IV at a height of 70 m
emerge from the forest.

**A pyramid reaching up to
the heavens**
Elevation of Temple II at Tikal,
dating from the eighth century:
the drawing underlines the
volumes of the high platforms.
The upper part of the *cresteria*
has been reconstructed in this
drawing; the original has been
eroded by vegetation.

Page 47
**A proud display on the
central square**
The lofty profile of Temple II of
Tikal dominates the great square
surrounded with sculpted stelae.
At the edge of the stairs that
lead up to the northern acropolis,
these commemorative monoliths
bear carvings and inscriptions
whose dates follow the events of
the seventh and eighth centuries.
Towards 830, the city's population
decreased and Tikal was abandoned early in the tenth century.

The lofty outline of the pyramid
Temple I, (around 50 m high) stands in the centre of the sacrificial centre of Tikal; it is a perfect example of the Mayan pyramid outlined against the tropical forest of Petén. The incline of the single central flight of steps that scale the temple's nine platforms in vertiginous: more than 70°.

Page 49
A ladder to the sky
At the back of the huge central square of Tikal, studded with commemorative stelae, Temple I rises in one bound to the celestial realm governed by the gods. Access to the sanctuary, midway between earth and heaven, was allowed only to priests performing sacrifices.

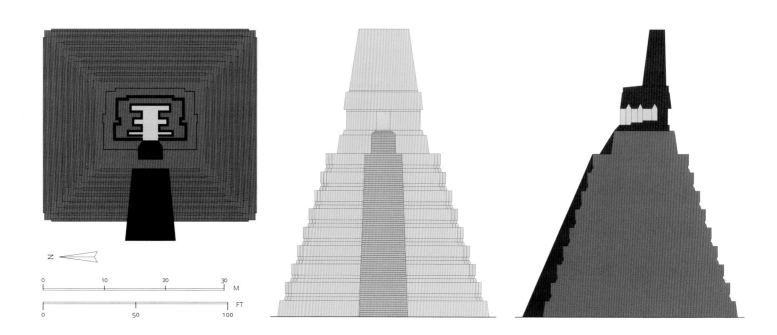

Limited interior spaces
Plan, elevation and section of Temple I of Tikal. In relation to the formidable mass of accumulated building materials, the internal space of the corbel-vaulted *cella* is tiny. The building went through several phases of construction.

sheer volume of work was therefore considerable. It was probably necessary to enlist hundreds, if not thousands, of workers all year round in order to build the permanent structures. Beyond the city, the Maya people continued to live in simple huts built of perishable materials on the city outskirts and in the surrounding agriculture zones.

The large number of tasks involved naturally required differing degrees of specialization. The unskilled workers would have been entrusted with the various menial jobs such as gathering suffcent combustible material for the manufacture of quicklime cutting stone in the quarries and transporting the stone to the building site. The rural "proletariat", that is those who found themselves unemployed at certain times of the year, could perform these tasks. Other tasks, which would have included cutting stone blocks in preparation for dressing, assembling the stone walls, sawing wood for lintels and for the interior decoration of the sanctuaries, called for skilled workers. And finally, teams of skilled artisans were needed: masons for the sculptural work, decorators for the stucco work, painters for the polychrome surfaces and scribes who were literate and thus capable of carving the inscriptions.

The above list does not encompass either the design or the architectural planning. Neither does it consider the question of the actual drawing and the execution of the blueprints. It does not tackle the matters of the siting and development of buildings that were cyclically renewed (that is by superimposing new structures on old). It confines itself to material details. Lastly, the rituals to be performed and the management of religions made a large body of clergy necessary. At their head was a ruler whose power was absolute.

A network of pyramids
The northern acropolis of Tikal forms a complex which, as a result of continual additions and superpositions over many centuries, never ceased to grow "organically" to form a symmetrical and rigorously organised whole.

A series of closely interlocking buildings form the mass of the central acropolis of Tikal. Built on several levels, they show that Mayan dignitaries were not afraid to build their homes above the cermonial squares.

The Role and Function of the Pyramids

The Maya pyramids fulfilled various functions. The major difference between a Mayan pyramid and an Egyptian one resides in the fact that the prime function of the former, like the Babylonian ziggurat, was to support a sanctuary; this was never the case with the Pharaonic pyramids. The Maya building is a monumental pedestal at whose summit stands the place of divine worship.

The pyramids of Tikal, in this context, can be seen to exalt the union between earth and heaven. They form an extraordinary "ladder" which allows the priests to ascend toward the highest heavens and communicate with the gods of the cosmos. By contrast, like the Egyptian pyramids, the base of the Mayan pyramids often concealed a tomb, either subterranean or housed within the built mass. It was there that the mortal remains of the deified ruler were laid to rest. This function only came to light in 1952. That year marked the discovery of the now celebrated crypt of the Temple of the Inscriptions at Palenque. In it lay the sarcophagus of Pacal. Thus the Mayan pyramid has a twofold importance, being at once a temple and a funerary monument.

But as the autocratic power of the master of each city gradually increased, and with it the tendency of certain great centres to impose their hegemony on neighbouring settlements, the religious and funerary functions fused in a glorification of personal power. The pyramids came to transcend their more strictly defined functions, and were built largely as a herculean assertion of the power of the city's ruler. And the stelae arranged on the esplanade at the foot of each temple proclaimed in writing the great deeds of each potentate's reign, recording his birth, his marriage, his victories, naming the enemies he sacrificed to the gods, and listing his achievements.

Maya architecture, seen in this perspective, became the instrument of individual glory: the king, as the person who dedicated altars, platforms and pyramids to divine powers, came to be very closely associated with the divinities that he honoured.

City Inscriptions

The ancient Maya city of Tikal, discovered in the eighteenth century, was first studied and excavated in 1881. The 500 km^2 that form the city's overall area has been the focus of many excavations and restoration projects. Its centre contains no less than 3 000 monuments in an area of 16 km^2. At the heart of this vast agglomeration, the so-called ceremonial zone which includes the principal pyramids, the ball courts and palace, covers an area 1 200 by 600 m. Here stand the giant sanctuaries of the north acropolis.

The complex, which dates back in great part to the sixth and seventh centuries, after a period of relative obscurity for Tikal, marks the renaissance of the capital of the Petén. It is arranged to a symmetrical design, oriented north/south, on an axis 200 m long with a width not exceeding 150 m. But in this area there are seventeen buildings, the most impressive of which rise to a height of 45 m.

At the back of the square Great Plaza, flanked left and right by the high pyramids christened Temple I and Temple II, a "forest" of commemorative stelae and sacrificial altars (around forty monoliths in all) stand before three further pyramids bearing the prosaic names of Temples 32, 33 and 34. These rise up before the visitor, followed by a small symmetrical *patio*, around which are arranged further smaller pyramids. It was in the Great Plaza that dynastic celebrations glorifying the power of the ruler of Tikal were held.

Even though the Maya sought to take advantage of the slightest mound or rise and the slightest fold in the generally flat terrain of the Petén to establish their acropolises, the complex here is level. There is no doubt that the complex is a carefully planned urbanistic whole, whose arrangement of individual features called for an elaborate building plan. The composition is governed equally by the requirements of the rituals, dedicated to the different gods, the hierarchy of the sanctuar-

A "forest of stelae"
On the central square of Tikal, monoliths record the history of the Mayan capital. They stand at the edge of the stairs in front of the northern acropolis.

The ceremonial centre
Schematic plan of the main buildings of Tikal:
 1. Temple I
 2. Temple II
 3. Temple III
 4. Temple V
 5. Group A: Main Square, between the northern acropolis and the central acropolis
 6. Group B: southern acropolis
 7. Group C: square of the seven temples
 8. Group D
 9. Group E
10. Group F
11. Group G
12. Processional causeway
13. Water reservoirs

Pottery with polychrome figures
These two cylindrical Mayan vases from Tikal depict scenes of audience: a high dignitary, sitting cross-legged on a stool that serves as a throne, receives the homage of his subjects. Height: 29.8 cm and 28.4 cm respectively. (Tikal, National Museum)

Young lord of Copán
This sculpted trachyte head shows the gentle expression of a Mayan lord, wearing a turban and large ear jewellery. The work is from the site of Copán (Honduras) and dates from the eighth century.

ies and the grand design of which the buildings commissioned by successive rulers formed part.

This subordination of great monuments to a unified plan in Maya culture indicates a long-term scheme which sometimes developed over several centuries. Indeed, a reading of the inscriptions now enables us, for the most part, to attribute to a specific person – whose name, like the date of his reign and their dynasty to which he belonged, is known to us – the construction of each monument and each tomb, as well as the erection of each stela. The history of the buildings reflects the events that affected the city. They relate the glorious episodes that followed collapse, rebellion and invasion.

The plan of Tikal also included large causeways linking different parts of the town, along which sumptuous processions must have taken place. It also included reservoirs – which were for the most part excavations resulting from the removal of rock from the open-cast quarries whence workers extracted the construction materials. Cisterns for drinking water were situated below the plazas and esplanades; they drained off surplus water, filling up during the rainy season.

Tikal is the most spectacular of the lowland cities of Petén and Belize. But the Maya towns of the Classic period can be counted in their dozens; besides Uaxactún and Cerros already mentioned, we should also list Nakum, Naranjo, Río Azul, Altun Ha, Xultún, amongst others. They all contain a multitude of buildings patiently exhumed by archaeologists from the dense layer of vegetation and humus. There are local variations, but almost all contain the pyramids, platforms, palaces, ball courts, stelae and altars that form the usual repertory of symbolic-religious monuments in Maya centres.

It would seem that these cities, groups of which comprised principalities under the power of a single ruler, enjoyed a certain autonomy at cultural and religious levels. The principalities frequently clashed in inter-tribal battles during which the prisoners taken were doomed to sacrifice.

But there were also strong links, based on cultural exchanges and thriving trade between these cities scattered in the rain forest. Commodities such as cocoa-pods and shells (conches) were traded between the lowlands and the high Mexican plateaus. Similarly, at the end of the Maya civilisation, the emergence of gold-working stemmed from commercial links brought about by the coastal trade that grew up between the Andean cultures and the Mexican civilisations, by way of the peoples of Central America.

The trade routes of these commercial contacts have been partly reconstructed. They often coincide with waves of migration that brought distant artistic influences into Maya territory, in particular in the field of architecture. Indeed, a feature first found in the great city of Teotihuacan, not far from present-day Mexico City, reached Tikal around A.D. 375. It was a time when Mexican influence was strongly felt. In this case, *talud-tablero* of Teotihuacan replaced the stepped levels of the pyramids. It consisted of a series of platforms, each with a sloping base like a rampart, over which projected a vertical panel framed by a moulding. This configuration, alternating a gradient steeper than 60° with a vertical surface, temporarily replaced the characteristic silhouette of the pyramids of Tikal.

Archaeologists have noted a sort of "hiatus" in the Tikal chronology after A.D. 534. Inscriptions – which elsewhere continue uninterrupted – disappeared completely. Simultaneously, great building projects became fewer and further between. In the Classic building sites, activity was not fully restored until the late sixth century. From that time onwards, the Maya world evolved towards its "golden age": population, buildings and stone inscriptions all began to proliferate.

In the seventh and eighth centuries, the city of Tikal must have been the site of a resplendent civilization. Part of our evidence for this is the discoveries made in the tomb of ruler Ah Cacao, uncovered in 1962 below Temple I, "Pyramid of the Great Jaguar". This tomb, which dates back to circa A.D. 734, when Ah Cacao's son acceded to the throne of Tikal, contained rich offerings of jade and shells, as well as pottery and carved bones featuring images of the gods in an extremely refined figurative style.

Such finds help us to visualize the existence of these Maya "nobles", with their dazzlingly white cotton apparel, their polychrome ceremonial robes, their headdresses made of brightly coloured feathers, their jade jewellery, and their priests performing sacrifices on stone altars in a cloud of copal smoke. To the accompani-

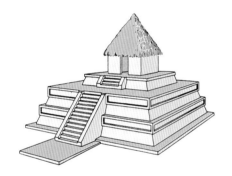

A memory of the northern plateaux
The influence of invading tribes from Teotihuacán made itself felt in Tikal with the introduction of the *talud-tablero* and its projecting vertical panels.

A huge complex
This model underlines the importance of the ceremonial centre of Tikal at its height (eighth century) and of the rigorous distribution of the pyramids built by the Mayan "clergy". (Guatemala City, National Museum of Archaeology and Ethnology)

Great stela of Quiriguá
The tallest Mayan monolith is on the site of Quiriguá, in the Río Motagua basin (Guatemala) and measures 10.66 m. This sandstone Stela E, erected in 771, weighs 65 tons. The sovereign is shown frontally, holding a small sceptre in his right hand and a tiny symbolic shield in his left. The detail of the face (right) shows him to be sporting a pointed goatee.

ment of horns and ritual chants, a whole nation thronged before the red pyramids amid the omnipresent tropical vegetation, which echoed with the cries of multi-coloured parrots, quetzals and toucans.

After the fateful date 869, which appears on the last Tikal stela, the history of the city came to an abrupt end.

In the Río Motagua Basin: Quirigúa and Copán

To the south-east of the country, in the mountainous terrain surrounding the Río Motagua basin, close to the current Guatemala–Honduras border, we find a province that wielded considerable influence in the urban civilization of the Classic Maya. In this area, set among the rocky folds of the Sierra Madre, the availability of rocks such as andesite and trachyte encouraged the pre-Columbian tribes to develop an art in which skilfully carved stone played a prominent role. In this province, the architecture features corbel vaults built in horizontal layers of dressed stone.

An important personnage
Dating from 775 – five years after
Stela E – Quiriguá's Stela C offers
a variation of the same Mayan
sovereign who captured the king
of Copán. The face, as is shown
by the detail (left), is identical,
adorned by the same goatee
beard; but the body is treated in
shallow relief, with the feet set
wide apart according to a stylistic
convention that one also finds in
Copán.

And there was a dramatic evolution in the field of sculpture: large stelae and altars
are found scattered liberally over the ancient sites.

These tendencies are particularly evident in two cities: Quiriguá and Copán. The
former, which is situated in the lower reaches of the Río Motagua, not far from
where it flows into the Gulf of Honduras and the Caribbean sea, is renowned for its
sculpted monoliths. The largest stela of the Maya world is to be found here: a block
of 10.6 m weighing no less than 65 tons. This Stela E, dated A.D. 771, stands in the
fertile plain. It was brought to the site along the irrigation channels that linked the
nearby hills with the town of Quiriguá. It was transported – like the Olmec blocks of
La Venta – by water, aboard rafts built of tree trunks from the rainforest.

At Quiriguá, the Great Plaza, oriented north/south, is dotted with stelae, each of
which was added at five-year intervals, from 746 to 810, the date at which all activity in the city seems to cease. The excellent sculpture exhibited in the stelae is a quality that they share with a remarkable series of monolithic altars. Altar Zoomorph P,

The colossal altars of Quiriguá
On the shores of Río Motagua, there is a series of strange sacrificial altars consisting of huge sculpted monoliths. Behind this coarse block (in the foreground), which the sculptor has been content to decorate with relief carvings without smoothing its surfaces, the enormous "Zoomorph" P, dating from 795, shows the Earth monster from whose jaws the sovereign emerges sitting cross-legged.

Below left
The penultimate date of Quiriguá
On this Stela K, faintly carved with plumed motifs, the sovereign of Quiriguá wears a crown like those worn by the kings of Piedras Negras. Dating from 805, this monolith is the penultimate chronological reference on the site.

Below right
In the image of the Prince
The Mayan stelae of Quiriguá all show a full-face high-relief portrait with a headdress of superposed masks

A formidable monolith
"Zoomorph" P, standing at 2.20 m is a transposition of the image of the giant cosmological tortoise. The back of the monolith represents the stylised face of the earth monster surrounded with glyphs. Various interpretations have been put forward to explain the symbolism of this rich, baroque decoration.

representing the Earth monster, is carved in a surprisingly "baroque" design, in which hieroglyphic signs and symbolic ornamentation mingle. In the centre, a human figure, sitting cross-legged, emerges from the fanged jaws of a terrifying monster. This regal figure wears an elaborate and sumptuous crown, and is represented full face in the cosmic grotto. This motif, a reworking of an Olmec formula, calls to mind a famous altar from La Venta exhibited at the Park-Museum of Villahermosa. The similarity may not be coincidental, although several centuries separate the two works: indeed, it was to the mountains bordering the Río Motagua basin that the Olmecs came to quarry a seam of green jade, a mineral of which they had made, long before the Maya did so, a symbol of rebirth and the afterlife.

The artistic autonomy of the Maya cities is evident to anyone who compares the styles of the various centres where stelae were produced: each site possessed its own style of expression. One cannot confuse a sculpture from Quiriguá (or Copán) – with its figure rendered full face in vigorous high relief carving – with, for example, a stela of Tikal, where the ruler is represented in profile in very low relief. Similarly, the highly structured decoration that surrounds the head of the principal figure at Quiriguá is limited to quasi-geometrical forms, whereas at Tikal, the hieratic scene records with meticulous precision each detail of the costume and ceremonial objects clasped by the holder of power.

Quiriguá, situated in the fertile plain on the edge of the river, never attained the size of Copán, on which it came to depend politically. However, a ruler of Copán, named 18-Rabbit was defeated in 738 by the king of Quiriguá.

A Man-made Acropolis

Copán figures amongst the most original of the Classic cities; though only 50 km from Quiriguá, it is situated in present-day Honduras. It dominates a hilly region irrigated by a tributary of the Río Motagua, the Río Copán. Indeed, during violent flooding, this river has eroded the acropolis which it passes to the east. In so doing, it has revealed the structure of the terrain by a sort of stratigraphic cross-section. It can be therefore observed that the ceremonial complex of Copán is in large part built on a vast man-made terrace.

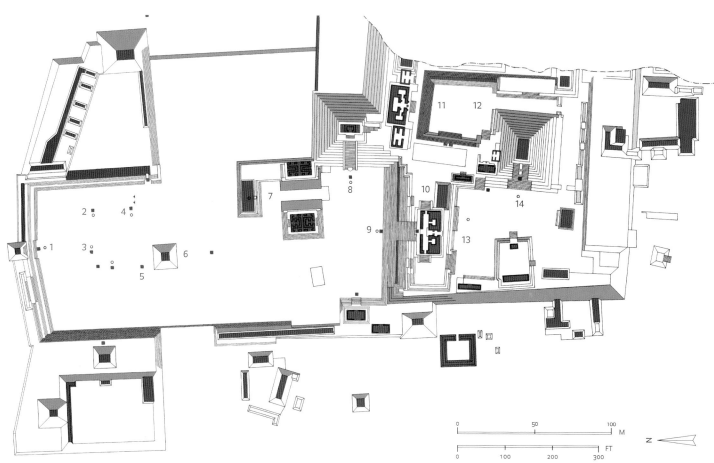

Page 61 above

Stela and altar of Copán

On the square in front of the ball court of Copán, a series of monoliths are scattered over the wide open space provided by the artificial substructure. The association of an altar with a stela (here the F Group, dating from 721) constitutes a characteristic ritual complex.

Page 61 below

Traces of colour on the stelae

As at Quiriguá, the sovereigns of Copán are depicted frontally on the great monoliths. Stela H, dating from 782, shows a rich sovereign, wearing sumptuous adornments of jade and feathers. The work, which bears traces of colour, shows the king emerging from the jaws of a stylized jaguar.

Page 60 above

A Mayan capital in Honduras

Copán numbers amongst the great cities of the Classic period: placed at the extreme south of Mayan territory, its golden age occurred around the year A.D. 700. The general view of the square shows, on the left, the ball court and its sloping banks and, on the right, the great hieroglyphic stairway climbing the main pyramid.

Page 60 below

An artificial square

Plan of the whole ceremonial centre of Copán in Honduras:
 1. Stela D
 2. Stela F
 3. Stela C
 4. Stela H
 5. Stela A
 6. Pyramid
 7. Ball court
 8. Hieroglyphic stairway
 9. Stela N and great Stairway
10. Stand
11. Building 22
12. Eastern court
13. Western court
14. Southern pyramid

The centre of the town is built inside a rectangle oriented on a north/south axis, 500 m long by 300 m wide (15 hectares), and is organised on an orthogonal ground plan. The major part of this area, carefully levelled and surrounded by earth banks on which platforms and pyramids stand, consists of man-made terraces; these materials were brought here by human hand. The Maya transported almost a million m^3 of building materials here in order to create the famous plaza, on which a dozen stelae stand; it attains a height of 30 m and a surface area of 3.5 hectares. The highest pyramidal structures dominate the level of the river by some 38 m.

Copán has been the subject, during this last decade, of a number of excavations and successful restorations. On the acropolis, in particular, the imposing Hieroglyphic Stairway – with some 2 500 sculpted signs on the risers of its 63 steps – was restored after the discovery of an underground tomb. This major inscription – the longest dynastic document known in the Maya region – deserves to be studied in depth. But the disorder introduced in the arrangement of certain hieroglyphics during the first archaeological expeditions renders the results difficult to interpret. We do know, however, that the dates listed range from 545 to 757. This monumental stairway, flanked by sloping string walls, leads to a small *cella* which formed the sanctuary of the pyramid.

To the south stands the imposing Structure 22 whose door depicts the entry to the Other World. It dominates the sunken eastern court, which is surrounded by tiers of seating. A series of grand stairways delimits the courts. They structure the complex of buildings crowning the acropolis.

At the top of a sweep of steps no less than 90 m wide, to the south of the Great Plaza, stands a curious monument consisting of a sanctuary. The back of this temple adjoins a palace, which overlooks the Spectators' Tribune, the western court. The tiered seating that runs along this Tribune also forms a hieroglyphic stairway.

Almost all the late period of this acropolis is the work of one ruler named Yax-Pac who reigned from 763 and remained on the throne for more than forty years. Stela 11 commemorates his apotheosis in 810, naming him "Father of the Nation". Shortly before the final decline of the Maya, this sovereign remodelled the group of buildings covering the acropolis of Copán. At this period, the majority of the Mayan cities in Guatemala had already entered into decline.

The gateway of hell
The entrance of Building 22 of Copán, dating from 764, shows on each side atlantean figures kneeling on bare skulls; they support a two-headed serpent representing the sky, its undulating coils resting on the lintel. This is a symbolic portrayal of the entrance to the Underworld.

Mathematics and the Maya Calendar

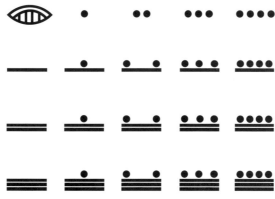

Dated inscriptions
The Pre-Columbian custom of dating inscriptions goes back to the Olmecs: on the left, this fragment of Stela C from the Olmec city of Tres Zapotes (Veracruz) represents the first known usage of the "Long Count" that the Maya later adopted. Already the figures are represented by points (1) and bars (5), according to the adjoining table. The date inscribed on the stela may correspond to 31 B.C. (Mexico City, National Museum of Anthropology)

Even before the most recent advances in the decipherment of Maya writing, specialists such as Spinden, Morley and Thompson had succeeded in reading inscriptions relating to the calendar. They also understood how the system of numeral notation worked. In this, they had been guided by the information provided in the middle of the sixteenth century by Bishop Diego de Landa, and by the very few manuscripts that escaped the destruction ordered by Bishop Landa in his desire to eradicate every trace of the native religions of the New World.

As indicated, the Maya were in possession of a numerical notation system based on dots (1) and bars (5); in addition, they used a positional system that presumes the existence of a "zero", combined with a vigesimal basis. This means that, in the first column of positional notation , the first 19 named numbers occur; in the following column appear 19 values of 20 etc. This system implies that columns are changed at 20, 400, 8000, 160 000 etc. In practical terms, the only exception to this system was the calculation of dates in the calendar; the chronological notations had to take account of the fact that the solar year was composed of 360 + 5 days (see below).

The Maya determined a date using two systems of calculation, one founded on the solar cycle of 365 days, divided into 18 months of 20 days (+ 5 days of festivities); the other on the sacred or divinatory calendar of 260 days, resulting in a notation of 13 numbers and 20 names. Their method of date transcription was therefore based on two variables whose original starting point only recurred after a cycle of 18 890 days, 52 years, or 73 sacred years, a length of time which, for many pre-Columbian peoples, was the equivalent of a sort of "century".

The method of notation called the Long Count, which the Maya used to date an event in their Classic inscriptions, relies on a system combining five figures; the *kin*, = 1 day; the *uinal*, = 20 days; the *tun*, = 18 times 20 days, = 360 days. 20 *tun* make one *katun*, or 7200 days; 20 *katun* equals one *baktun* of 144 000 days, or 394.5 solar years.

To decipher a date made of five figures, for example, 9.13.16.5.8., the elements should be added up thus:

9 *baktun*	of	144 000 days	=	1 296 000 days
13 *katun*	of	7 200 days	=	93 600 days
16 *tun*	of	360 days	=	5 760 days
5 *uinal*	of	20 days	=	100 days
8 *kin*	of	1 day	=	8 days

or in all 1 395 468 days, the equivalent of around 3 823 years. In the "Long Count", the system returned to its original position only after a cycle of 374 440 years. If one accepts the usual correlation with the Christian calendar, the start of the computation (0 *baktun*) goes back to 3116 B.C.

From the eighth century (the late Classic period), the Maya tended to simplify their chronological notations. In place of the "Long Count", which requires five glyphs, they used only three glyphs. The date then consisted of the number of *katun*, the number of the "month", and the number of the day.

This vigesimal notation permitted the calculation of very long periods of time: thus, the *baktun* of 144 000 days could be multiplied by 20, then again by 20 (or 400), and again by 20 (8 000) and a last time by 20 again (160 000), which is equivalent to a *alautun* representing 23 billion 40 million days – that is to say, more than 63 million years. It is hard to imagine how a Greek or Roman could have transcribed such large numbers. These huge figures occurred in the mode of calculation that the Maya applied to their astronomical observations.

The Golden Age of Palenque

Flourishing of the Arts in Chiapas

Page 67

The beauty of a face
A typical profile of a ruler of Palenque, with his artificial nasal ridge, extending right up to the middle of his forehead – a feature of the Mayan canon of beauty. Detail from the Panel of the Slaves, dating from A.D. 730. (Palenque, Museum of Palenque)

The western zone of Maya territory called Chiapas is bounded to the north-east by the Usumacinta river – forming the frontier between Mexico and Guatemala – and to the west by the Rio Grijalva crossing a region once occupied by the Olmecs, they converge before flowing into the Gulf of Mexico. At the end of the Preclassic period (400–250 B.C.), the Olmec nation played a major part in civilizing the tribes that came into contact with it.

The lush wetlands of Chiapas are dotted with ancient cities whose ruins have been invaded by the tropical forest. Seventy Maya cities have been recorded, the most important of which, apart from Palenque, are Yaxchilán on the banks of the Usumacinta, Bonampak and Tonina, Teapa and Simojovel, and Jonuta and Comalcalco to the west. On the Guatemalan side of the Usumacinta, we should also mention the city of Piedras Negras, built in a similar style.

In the heart of this land of rain forest and marsh, criss-crossed by rivers, Palenque is perhaps the most inspiring of the great Classic cities built in Chiapas by the Maya. With its back to the foothills of the Sierra Madre and their dense plant-cover, the town stands on a shelf-like area with a far-reaching view to the north. To the south, it is bounded by a series of escarpments, whose lower summits are covered with buildings. The Rio Otolum, a small tributary of the Usumacinta, flows through the ruins. Because it threatened to erode the constructions when in spate, the Maya diverted its course by means of an underground conduit in the vicinity of the great ceremonial buildings.

Huts covered an expanse of around 6 km, while the zone built in stone measured 2 000 m east-west and 1 000 m north-south. Within this perimeter, the principal monuments – pyramids, palaces, ball courts – were grouped mainly around a Great Plaza surrounded by a palace building with several courtyards and the Temple of the Inscriptions. Adjoining this main group, the complex of the Temple of the Cross lies to the east and the group of the Temple of the Count to the north; these mark the limits of the ceremonial area.

An Eighteenth Century Discovery

Palenque was one of the first sites in the Maya world to be explored. As early as 1789, Charles III, King of Spain, – who had been intrigued by the ruins of Pompeii when he was King of Naples and the Two Sicilies – ordered a soldier of fortune, one Antonio del Río, to lead an expedition to Palenque. The expedition took place in 1787, and the works carried out at that time mark the beginning of the archaeological investigations of pre-Columbian civilization. They were greeted with incomprehension and the results were not published until 1822.

Later, Charles IV of Spain commissioned "Colonel" Guillaume Dupaix to lead an exploratory mission together with the Mexican artist Luciano Castañeda. The two men visited the city in 1805–1806. They brought back drawings of limestone and stucco shallow relief carvings. This material appeared in Paris only in 1834, under the title of *Antiquités mexicaines*.

Superposed gods
A terracotta incense-burner from Palenque: this long ceramic tube, decorated with deities stacked one above the other, was used for the offerings of copal that the priests made during ceremonies. (Villahermosa, Tabasco Museum)

Then in 1821, Johann-Friedrich Maximilian von Waldeck spent some time at the site. A brilliant draughtsman – he was a pupil of David – Waldeck made invaluable surveys. But, like his predecessors del Rio and Dupaix, he burned the surrounding vegetation in order to get a better view of the ruins. He was not the only explorer to do this, but his action caused irreparable damage to the polychrome decoration. His work only saw the light of day forty-four years later in 1866, as he was unable to elicit sufficient interest in France for the pre-Columbian peoples.

The emergence of Palenque from obscurity can be attributed to two men – the American "reporter" John L. Stephens and the accomplished English artist Frederick Catherwood. The accuracy of Catherwood's drawings is due to the fact that he worked with the aid of a *camera lucida*, a device that foreshadowed the camera. The resulting book, *Incidents of Travel in Central America,* which appeared in New York in 1842, was a veritable triumph. It gave a romantic and yet accurate image of a whole series of Maya sites.

Several scientific missions to Palenque followed, during which the sites were cleared and the restoration of the main buildings undertaken. One of the most remarkable finds of pre-Columbian archaeology – the funeral crypt discovered in 1952 by Alberto Ruz – not only revealed exceptional treasures and sanguinary funerary rites but also overthrew many of the notions then prevailing about the most advanced people of Mesoamerica.

Palenque occupies a prime position in the history of the decipherment of Mayan writing, due to the fact that the city, with its temples and its crypt, contains a large

The Temple of Inscriptions
In the heart of the city of Palenque (Chiapas), dominating the Mayan site, stands the Temple of Inscriptions, where the tomb of a king called Pacal, who reigned between 615 and 683, was discovered. Climbing the platforms of the building, the central stairway leads to the top sanctuary composed of five bays giving access to the vestibule and the *cella* from which a hidden staircase plunges down to a funerary crypt in the body of the building.

Below the foothills
Standing on the first foothills of the Sierra Madre, the site of Palenque dominates the featureless plain of Chiapas that extends as far as the Usumacinta delta. On the left, the Temple of the Inscriptions; on the right, the Great Palace and its tower.

Overall plan of the main monuments of Palenque:
 1. Temple of the Cross
 2. Temple of the Foliated Cross
 3. Temple of the Sun
 4. Temple of the Inscriptions
 5. Great Palace
 6. Structure XIII
 7. Structure XI
 8. Ball court
 9. Temple of the Count
10. Northern group

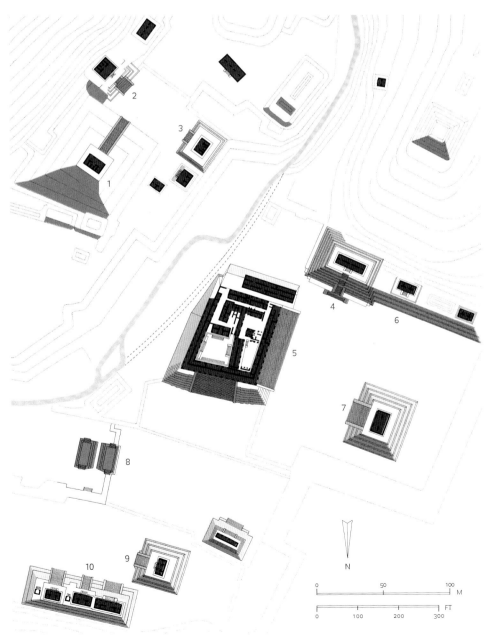

Surrounded by the rain forest
The monuments in the centre of Palenque seen from the air: on the left below, the mass of the Great Palace and its courtyards; to the left above, the group of the Temple of the Sun and Temple of the Foliated Cross; to the right, the Temple of the Inscriptions. The burgeoning plant-life on all sides threatens to overwhelm the site.

number of hieroglyphic inscriptions. These rich assets, only recently explained by specialists (see *A Forest of Kings* by Linda Schele and David Friedel, 1990), have now made it possible to answer a whole host of questions relative to this Classic city and the genesis of its monuments.

For until the Mayan glyphs were deciphered and it became possible to date the buildings of the religious centre, the chronology of buildings and rulers was obscure.

The Buildings of Palenque

For a visitor, the arrival at Palenque is spectacular. The long road winds uphill and leads to a Great Plaza flanked to the south by steep hills, covered in giant trees and thick tropical creeper. To the right stand three pyramids. The third and most im-pressive pyramid seems to project its central stairway up the eight steeply raised terraces to the sanctuary that stands on its own platform at the summit. This is the famous Temple of the Inscriptions. Deep within it has the funerary crypt of a powerful seventh-century sovereign: Pacal. It was discovered along with Pacal's treasure and mortal remains in 1952. Thanks to Linda Scheele and David Friedel, we can now pronounce his name.

The palace stands opposite. Its wide staircase leads to a pillared gallery covered by a concrete stepped vault. Behind this façade – forming a right-angle with the pyramid – stands a high tower topped with a stonework roof which bears some resemblance to a four-cornered hat. This palace forms a rectangular complex containing three patios surrounded by galleries.

Penetrating further into the site, we reach the level above the Great Plaza, where we come upon a group of temples on the far bank of the Rio Otolum, their sanctuaries surmounted by large *cresteriaes*. They surround a *plaza*: to the left is the Temple of the Cross, preceded by a long sweep of steps ascending the levels of the recently restored pyramid on which it stands: to the rear stands the Temple of the Foliated Cross and, opposite it, the Temple of the Sun.

Lastly, below the Great Plaza, beyond the ball court and before reaching the relatively delapidated north Group, stands the Temple of the Count which has recently been restored.

Such is the centre of Palenque. The surrounding hills are also covered with buildings, though these have not yet been excavated.

At Palenque, a very specific style of architecture flourished, characterised in particular by the shape of the concrete roof-coverings which resemble mansard roofs. The ornamentation, consisting of high relief stucco features, sometimes modelled in the round, must, in combination with the vivid painted polychromy, have imparted sumptuous appearence to the religions and ceremonial buildings.

An exceptional pyramid
Plan, elevation, and longitudinal and transversal section of the Pyramid of Inscriptions at Palenque: the double flight of stairs descending from the top sanctuary down to the underground funerary crypt is a unique configuration in the Classic Mayan world.

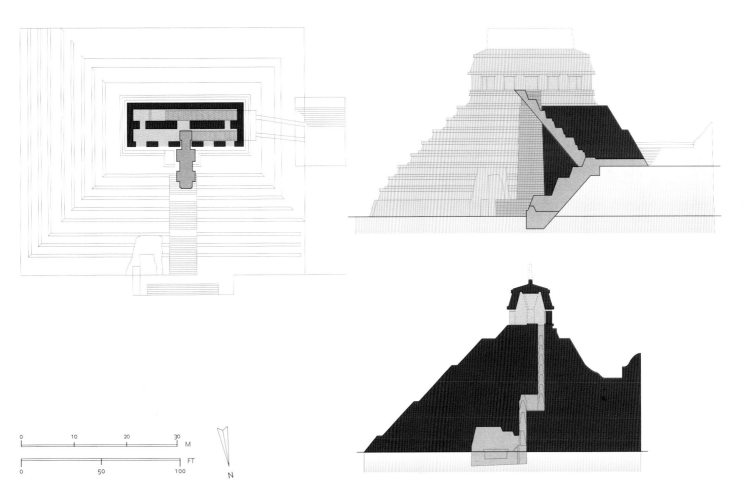

0   10   20   30 M

0   50   100 FT

N

A King Named Pacal

A striking face
A portrait of Pacal, the sovereign who reigned almost seventy years over Palenque: this stucco head is a youthful representation of the king. The nasal ridge stands out in relief on his forehead. (Mexico City, National Museum of Anthropology)

Pacal has already been mentioned – a name that the decipherment of Maya texts revealed to specialists around twenty years ago. We know about this King of Palenque from a series of dates inscribed in his funerary crypt. He was born in A.D. 603 and his mother was called Lady Zak Kuk. In 615, at the age of twelve, he acceded to the throne of Palenque. In 635, the birth of his son Chan Bahlum (or Jaguar Serpent) was announced. In carvings he is represented as possessing six fingers and six toes, an anomaly that was very probably interpreted as a sign of divinity.

In 640, Pacal's mother died, and in 641 Chan Bahlum was designated as heir presumptive to the throne. The son was to wait more than four decades before succeeding the father, since Pacal reigned until the venerable old age of eighty. In 643, Pacal's father, Kan Bahlum Mô, died. It was in 647 that the king inaugurated his first sanctuary, which bore the name Temple of the Count.

The reign of Pacal, marked by ceremonies and sacrifices whose dates are scrupulously reported, was already well-advanced when, in 675, the sovereign decided to build the Temple of the Inscriptions. He chose to make this edifice his tomb. Eight years later, in 683, the octogenarian died. His son, Chan Bahlum, was almost fifty years old in 684 when he acceded to the throne, announcing ten days of feasting. He died in 702 after reigning over the city of Palenque for a period of eighteen years.

It transpires from the inscriptions that these two individuals, whose combined period of rule spanned the seventh century, were the builders of almost all the significant buildings of the city: to Pacal we owe the Temple of the Count, a large part of the complex that constitutes the Royal Palace, the Temple of the Inscriptions and its crypt. His son Chan Bahlum was responsible for the complex of the Temple of the Cross and the pyramids that surround it.

A descent towards the unknown
The staircase leading to the crypt
of the Pyramid of Inscriptions
is covered by a succession of
corbelled vaults. On the right, a
stonework conduit follows the
line of the steps leading towards
the light: it allowed the soul of
the dead man to communicate
with the world of the living.

Ancestral under protection
Ancestors in ritual garb –
quetzal-feather headdress,
figurine-sceptre and small,
symbolic shield – mounted
guard over Pacal's remains
(according to Alberto Ruz).

The Temple of the Inscriptions and its Crypt

Unlike the pyramids of Tikal, which contain only a minute *cella* on the huge stepped base, the Temple of the Inscriptions of Palenque is dominated by its sanctuary. This feature dictates the rectangular shape of the eight-stepped substructure culminating in a platform almost twice as wide as it is deep. On it a sanctuary of 22 by 7 m stands. The holy of holies, which may be entered through three doorways, is situated behind the five bays of the entrance portico with its high concrete vault. The sanctuary is covered with a typical mansard-style roof. The *cresteria* that once surmounted it today lies in ruins.

This stonework pyramid, with an outer stone cladding that probably bore a layer of polychromed stucco, reached 36 m at the top of the *cresteria*. The pillars of the temple's porticoed gallery are decorated with stucco images. Among the still recognizable standing figures is an effigy of the heir to the throne, Chan Bahlum, who completed his father's tomb.

Underneath the stone slabs that cover the top platform, Alberto Ruz Lhuillier discovered the first steps of a stairway which was walled up and filled with rubble. 300 tons of rubble and masonry obstructing the entrance had to be removed. The stairway led via two flights of vaulted steps down to the crypt situated in the lower part of the pyramid. The importance of this find made 26 m below the floor of the top sanctuary cannot be overemphasized: behind a triangular stone door which had to be pivoted, Ruz discovered a chamber that was almost totally filled by an enormous sarcophagus. This was covered by a sculpted slab 3.8 by 2.2 m weighing no less than 5.5 tons. The monolithic container itself weighed around 15 tons. This huge object, which could never have been transported along the narrow staircase of the crypt, had been set in the centre of the pyramid during the early stages of the monuments's construction.

Buried under the pyramid
The funerary crypt where King Pacal slept in his sarcophagus of stone with his treasures: under the powerful vaults that support the bulk of the Pyramid of Inscriptions, the monolithic sarcophagus was covered by a huge slab weighing 5.5 tons, decorated in symbolical relief carvings. On the right, a historical document: the Crypt of Palenque on the day it was opened, the 13 June 1952.

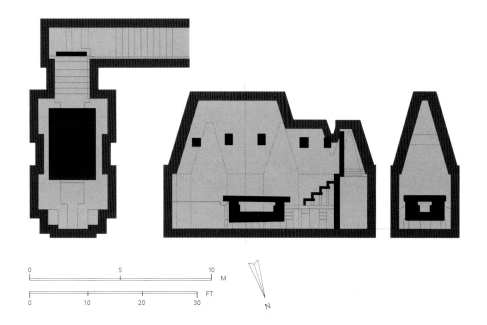

A skilful technique
Plan, elevation and longitudinal and transversal section of the funerary crypt in the centre of the Pyramid of Inscriptions in Palenque (late seventh century). The crossings of the corbelled vaults form a ingenious buttressing system against the weight of masonry that threatened to crush the chamber.

Adorned with feathers

A second portrait of king Pacal in stucco was discovered under the base of his sarcophagus in the crypt of Palenque: it shows the sovereign in the tranquillity of his mature years, mid-seventh century. Here too, the ornament linking of the bridge of the nose to the forehead conforms to the Mayan canons of beauty. (Mexico City, National Museum of Anthropology)

Pacal's funerary mask

Entirely made of jade mosaic, this funerary mask, 24 cm high, representing the ruler of Palenque, was placed over the face of the deceased king. With eyes made of shells, mother of pearl and obsidian, it is composed of nearly 200 pieces, carefully reconstructed by the team of the archaeologist Albert Ruz. Situated in the mouth of the dead man, the emblem in the form of a T is a protective amulet. (Mexico City, National Museum of Anthropology)

It is here that the remains of Pacal, King of Palenque, lay surrounded by his treasure, bejewelled amulets, as well as his stucco portraits sculpted in the round. Lastly, an extraordinary mask in jade mosaic was found still in place over the face of the dead man.

The chamber of the crypt itself attests to the virtuosity of Maya architects: in order to lessen the risks of collapse due to the considerable weight of the pyramid (more than 50 000 tons), they designed a space – in the form of the traditional hut – whose ground plan presents recessed transversal buttresses at both ends. These niches formed veritable transepts intended to consolidate the walls of the crypt. This formula, which combined cross vaulting, producing niches that strengthened the walls, with recessed buttresses re-enforcing the roof, proves the ingenuity of the Maya builders at the end of the seventh century.

We should lastly mention the dramatic surprise awaiting the discovers of the crypt of Palenque: on the ground at the entrance of the chamber lay the skeletons of five individuals of both sexes. These victims had been ritually sacrificed and were intended to accompany the dead king into the afterlife, the dwelling place of the dead that the Maya called Xibalba.

The Treasures of the Crypt

Among the works of art contained in the crypt of the Temple of the Inscriptions, we should first and foremost mention the lid of Pacal's sarcophagus. On this huge slab of more than 8 m² is a cosmological design whose motifs offer a paradigm of Mayan spiritual themes.

At its centre, the bas-relief represents the sovereign Pacal lying on top of the earth monster. He is tilted backwards, as if transfixed in ecstasy, with his face raised to the heavens. Underneath him, the gaping mouth of the underworld, symbolized by the jaws of a jaguar, makes ready to swallow up the dead king. Above the sovereign stands the Cosmic Tree, in the form of a cross, with depictions of the Dragon at its extremities, symbolizing blood, the primordial element in Mayan ritual, as in the majority of pre-Columbian religions.

This tree is surmounted by the Celestial Bird: a variety of quetzal or Phoenix that reigns over the heavens. Suspended from this Tree of Life, like a garland, is a Serpent with a head at each end. Its jaws, suspended on either side, are wide open and the heads of two divinities emerge from them.

In short, the whole Maya pantheon, with its cosmological system, is summed up by this magnificent bas-relief sculpture. The work's extraordinary finesse and confidence contribute to its symbolic function; it teaches us about the organization of the universe. The days and nights, the stars including the Sun and Moon, and the Milky Way itself, form the frame (in the literal sense) of this *imago mundi* organized around the king. In the centre, Pacal plays the role of omnipotent ruler of the world of the quick and the dead, an intermediary between the chasm of Xibalba and the celestial lights. He lies as if suspended between two infinite states of being, the Lord of a mythical and divine universe.

Around the sarcophagus are carved representations of Pacal's ancestors. These family portraits link him to a whole royal lineage going back six generations. Inside the monolithic sarcophagus, in addition to a collection of green stone jewellery charms, the superb funerary mask in intensely coloured jade mosaic, that once covered the face of the dead king, restores his immortal appearance: the whites of his eyes made of mother-of-pearl, with irises of obsidian and painted pupils, give him a mesmerizing expression. In his mouth shines the amulet of immortality in the form of a "T". The bridge of his nose is emphasized – as on the bas-reliefs – by a facial decoration that rises to the middle of his forehead, in keeping with an aesthetic

**Dominated by the hill
of the "Mirador"**
At Palenque, the three temples
of the Group of the Cross – the
Temple of the Foliated Cross
(672), the Temple of the Cross
(692) and the Temple of the Sun
(690) – are built on pyramidal
substructures. Created by Pacal's
son, called Chan Bahlum, they all
possess a small *cella* covered
with a mansard-style roof,
surmounted by a *cresteria*.

The result of a recent restoration
A large centre stairway leads, in
six separate flights, to the Temple
of the Cross in Palenque. A recent
reconstruction has restored
its stately progress up to the
sanctuary; it had collapsed under
the weight of invading vegetation.

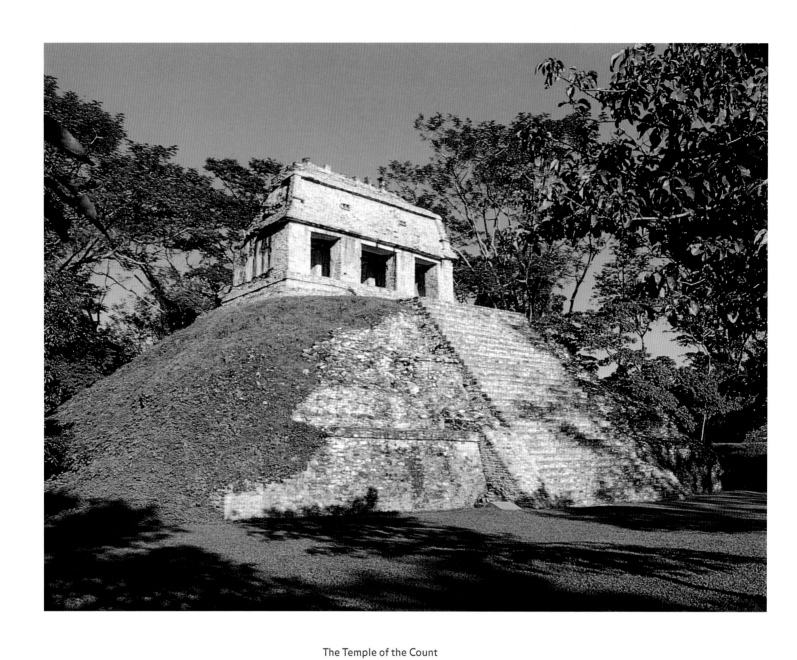

The Temple of the Count
In the northern group, the small
temple built on top of a pyramid
with a single central staircase
dates from the beginning of
Pacal's reign. It has recently
been partially restored.

The Temple of the Sun

Dating from 690, this sanctuary, typical of the style of Palenque, is notable for the *cresteria* that crowns its roof. The sloping sides of the mansard-style roof were covered in stucco reliefs. These have been damaged both by vegetation and the fires lit by the nineteenth-century explorers seeking to free the buildings from the jungle.

An ingenious structure

The section showing the Temple of the Sun displays the system of crossed vaults first perfected for the crypt of Palenque and applied in the Group of the Cross. Two oblong chambers form the "transepts" that are linked by a central "nave". In order to withstand the wind, the two sides of the *cresteria* lean one against the other, leaving a space in the centre.

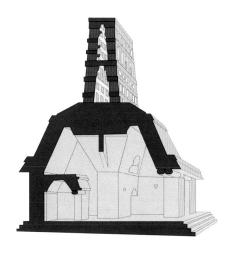

tradition exclusive to the Maya. We may suppose that this decoration was made of some form of plastic-like material – a derivative of latex which abounded in the rain forest – and applied to the skin.

Underneath the sarcophagus, archaeologists found two stucco heads of remarkable quality. These sculptures depict fine features, emphasized by extremely refined modelling which emphasizes the emaciated faces, the clear outline of the eyes and the subtle edging of the lips. These are true portraits of the sovereign at two periods of his life. They convey the idealized beauty of the great lord Pacal who reigned for sixty-eight years over the destiny of the city of Palenque.

The Complex of the Temple of the Cross

To the east of the Temple of the Inscriptions, the three other pyramids surveying a raised square are the work of Pacal's son, Chan Bahlum. They are, to the north, the south-facing Temple of the Cross (A.D. 692), the west-facing Temple of the Foliated Cross, twenty years older (672) and lastly the Temple of the Sun (690) opposite. These three edifices display the same architectural characteristics as the funerary crypt, that is to say, cross vaults. These allow the builders to enlarge the space formed by two chambers placed one behind the other without weakening it; the two chambers thus gain in unity. The almost square temple that stands on the highest level in each case comprises a three-bay portico resting on pillars. The façade and sloping roof were ornamented with stucco mouldings. Behind this vestibule, a wide central opening leads to a second chamber in which a sort of tabernacle stands. This inner chapel has the appearance of a *naos* and constitutes the sanctuary proper.

At the back of the holy of holies stand fine reliefs sculpted in pale limestone. Their style is akin to that of Pacal's sarcophagus. Ritual and mythological scenes are depicted, in which the gods participate side by side with Pacal and Chan Bahlum.

The cross vaults introduced at Palenque allow the creation of an elegant link between the two chambers of the temples, thanks to a sort of central linking nave perpendicular to the transversal vaulting. Here the progress toward the creation of better-unified internal spaces is evident. However, this feature is not found in later Mayan architecture, with the possible exception of certain chambers in the Toltec centre of Chichén Itzá.

Again we should draw attention to the lofty decorative structures crowning these temples: the *cresteria* is usually formed by two honeycombed walls buttressing each other. Their structure, made more delicate by lights, served as a base for stucco reliefs. These projecting sculptures depicted rulers and divinities. The *cresteria* thus played a role similar to that of the narrative pediments that ornament classical Greek temples.

The Great Palace and its Courtyards

The palace of Palenque is a vast raised construction that extends 85 m from north to south and 60 m from east to west (some 5 000 square m). It stands on a base covered by sweeping flights of steps on three sides: north, west and south. The base is in fact constituted by a pre-existing building, over which king Pacal built the current palace.

All around the perimeter of the palace there stood galleries open to the outside. A large proportion of these have survived. These porticoes were supported by pillars with a mansard-style roof in stonework. The outer sides of the rectangular pillars were originally covered in polychrome stucco, depicting scenes of palace rituals. Behind a partition wall, designed to support the heavy cement vaults, an-

The internal space of the temple
Inside the Temple of the Sun at Palenque, the Mayan roof formula – a corbelled vault in concrete – finds its most evolved expression with the crossings buttressing each other. Here, the porch of the temple is lit by the portico (on the right), with the entrance to the inner sanctum on the left.

The Great Palace of Palenque
Seen from the top of the Pyramid of Inscriptions, the Great Palace displays its porticoes separated by *patios* overlooked by the three-storey tower. Wide sweeps of steps lead up to the main façades, that are surrounded by pillared galleries. Most of the roofs have lost their *cresteria*. The group was built in the seventh and eighth centuries.

The remains of stucco decoration
The square pillars and the roofs of the Great Palace of Palenque were covered in a sculpted stucco decor painted in vivid colours.

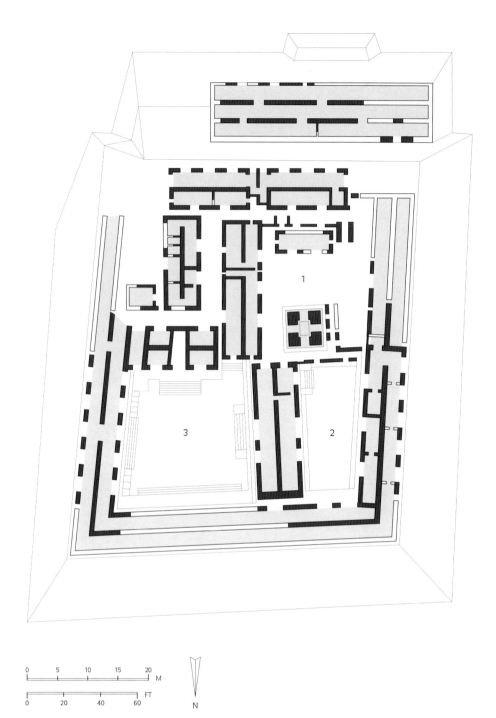

A complex structure
Plan of the Great Palace at Palenque, with its galleries surrounding the interior courtyards:
1. Tower
2. Western court
3. Great square

other gallery runs parallel. This looks onto the inner courtyards, around which the building is arranged. To the northwest, the long narrow western Patio itself contains a lower courtyard. To the north-east, the Great Patio is bordered on all four sides by stairways delimiting its wide sunken quadrangle. To the southwest, lastly, a third patio contains the four-storey tower, which is built entirely of stonework with strong corner pillars. This tower was, it seems, intended as a watchtower, for use in times of conflict with neighbouring tribes. Certain authorities maintain that it was an astronomical observatory facilitating the view of the horizon so that the rising of the stars could be observed. However, other constructions built on top of nearby hilltops – like structure XXIV, for example – would probably have served this purpose better.

Inside the palace, many rooms were given over to the residence of the ruler, his

Open towards the light
A central gallery in the Great Palace of Palenque, with its pillars and bays, above which beams of sapodilla supported the weight of the Mayan concrete roof. Below is a hieroglyphic stairway flanked by ramps.

family and friends. The underground quarters were probably used for storage, while the galleries and patios were employed for the pomp and circumstance of court festivals. The Great Court, in particular, with its decoration of monolithic stelae depicting standing figures set against the string walls, and its friezes in the style of leaning upright stones, conjures up the atmosphere of sumptuous palatial ceremonies.

Like the temples, the corbel vaults of the palace of Palenque display clear technological progress: the structures were made lighter by hollowing out the internal surfaces. These attempts to render the construction less heavy made it possible to reduce the volume of material used, without weakening the strength of the vaults. They thus served to optimize the material yield of the site. Palenque may therefore be considered an architectural experiment of great significance.

The seventh century, in the time of Pacal and Chan Bahlum, also marks the heyday of the great scenes depicted in bas-relief sculpture and of polychrome stucco decoration. These panels, covered in court personalities, divinities and a multitude of hieroglyphic signs, have contributed a great deal to our understanding of the dynasties, the history and the gods of the Maya.

Yaxchilán, on the Banks of the Usumacinta

Situated inside a loop of the Usumacinta river, the city of Yaxchilán spreads along the bank and onto the foothills, whose steep slopes directly overlook the river. During the Classic period, the Usumacinta became a channel of communications and trade between the cities of the Petén and Chiapas. In addition, Yaxchilán occupied a key position – as did its neighbour Piedras Negras, some 40 km downstream, on the Guatemalan bank – in the relations struck up between the various tribes of the

Subjugated peoples
On the great limestone reliefs (1.50 m high) running along the base of the galleries in the north-eastern courtyard of the Palace of Palenque, the tribal chiefs make their vows of allegiance. The style of these reliefs contrasts with the finesse of the interior panels.

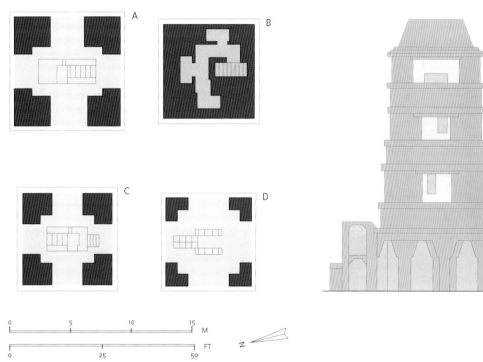

A surprising structure
Plan on four levels, elevation and section of the tower above the Great Palace of Palenque:
A First floor
B Mezzanine
C Second floor
D Third floor

Page 91
Observing the skies or man?
Was the high three-storey tower that overlooks the Great Palace complex intended for astronomical observations or to keep watch over the plain and prevent a surprise attack? What-ever the answer, it is unique in the Classic Mayan world.

**Begging the mercy
of the sovereign**
This detail from the leaning stelae
placed around the edge of the
north-east courtyard of the Palace
displays the submissive expression
of a tribal chief from the area
around Palenque. In order to
stress his importance, the artist
has portrayed him wearing the
insignia of power.

Kneeling before his master
With his head thrown back, this
vanquished figure's survival
depends on the magnanimity of
the King of Palenque. This large
stela of the Palace courtyard
underlines in almost caricature-
fashion the humility of the subject
who has come to beg for mercy.

Maya community: marriages between ruling dynasties, festivals celebrated in common, and exports of precious commodities and craft products.

The city of Yaxchilán – accessible today only by means of small aircraft landing on a makeshift runway – must have been vast. Its centre covers 1 km by 600 m and includes dozens of buildings – pyramids, palaces and ball courts. The buildings are scattered over a series of acropolises, some of which stand around 50 m or so above the river. Alas, owing to the difficulty of access, it has not yet been possible to bring in the machinery and manpower needed to clear and restore the ceremonial centre. Most of the buildings therefore remain submerged under vegetation.

Its architectural sculpture, however, makes Yaxchilán one of the best documented sites. For the interior surface of the lintels dominating the doors of the sanctuaries is, from a historical point of view, decorated with extremely refined carvings, accompanied by long hieroglyphic inscriptions. The dynasty that came to the throne in A.D. 320 became particularly eminent under its rulers "Shield-Jaguar" and "Bird-Jaguar", whose reigns covered the ninety years between 681 and 771.

Yaxchilán occupied an ideal position, and during these two reigns it gained most of its monuments. But its eminence was briefly overshadowed by the victory that

A carving of the accession to the throne
This detail from a limestone panel in the Great Palace of Palenque dating from 721, shows the king Kan-Xul sitting cross-legged on a stool in the form of a ceremonial rod with a head at each end. He prepares to receive the crown from his distant ancestor Pacal (who does not appear here). Wearing a solar pectoral, the king is not yet clothed in his state attire. (Palenque, Museum of Palenque)

The Wall Paintings of Bonampak

Found by American explorers in 1946, the paintings that decorate the interior walls of a palace at Bonampak, around 50 km to the south of Yaxchilán, represent a major discovery. They teach us that Maya artists were masters of pictorial techniques and possessed remarkable skills.

In three chambers situated side by side, the carefully stuccoed walls and vaults were covered in complex, highly-coloured scenes. They depict a ruler of Bonampak with his court, his warriors, his "nobles" and his priests. It relates an historic episode, recounting a battle and the ceremonies that marked the victory in A.D. 790 of the forces of Bonampak. In particular, we see the triumph of Lord Chan Muan, who had succeeded to the throne in 776 and whose wife was from Yaxchilán. These paintings not only glorified the processions of high dignitaries, with their standard-bearers, warriors and musicians, but also showed the captured and tortured enemy, as well as the human sacrifices organized to honour the gods.

The original paintings of Bonampak have unfortunately suffered terribly from the ambient humidity against which they had been protected for centuries by the mass of earth and vegetation obstructing the doors of the palace. As soon as they came into contact with the air, they lost their rich hues, and are of little value today. Fortunately, there is a series of copies made by Agustin Villagra Caleti and displayed in a building identical to the original in the Museum of Anthropology and History in Mexico City.

The value of this Classic painting, full of life and splendour, in many respects surpasses the art of narrative pottery, though the scenes that cover the sides of polychrome vases and goblets are of excellent quality. At Bonampak, we discover a monumentality and a sense of space that form an extension of the architecture. Just as mediaeval and Renaissance frescoes in the West attest to the piety and pomp of the societies in which they were produced, so the wall paintings of Bonampak offer a faithful reflection of the lavish, warlike existence of the Maya tribes. Better than bas-reliefs, stucco statuary or stelae, they teach us about the festivities, rituals, ceremonies, costumes, materials and weapons of the Maya. They are an expression of daily life at the court of the rulers during the Classic period. As such, they help us to imagine the palatial rooms and halls in all the splendour of their vivid colours, and they endow Maya monuments with a splendour that the ruins as discovered had not led us to expect.

The Bonampak "frescoes"
The western end of the first painted chamber of Bonampak, dating from around 790, shows, on the upper register, the king Chan Muan enthroned with his family; below, the major figures of the realm walk in a procession. (Mexico City, replica in the National Museum of Anthropology)

Elegance of style
An enlarged detail from a Mayan vase of the Classic period allows us appreciate the skill of draughtsmanship and the vivacity of expression of this woman painted on a bowl of the Classic period. (Barcelona, Barbier-Mueller Museum)

A haughty profile
On the other side of the same
bowl from Alta Verapaz,
macrophotography shows the
lively character of Mayan drawing
and the skill of the artist who,
like the painter of Bonampak,
here achieves a high degree of
virtuosity. (Barcelona, Barbier-
Mueller Museum)

Above right
High-ranking Mayan dignitaries
In the second chamber of the
palace of Bonampak, one side
shows (above) a standing group of
high-ranking dignitaries, and
(below) seated negotiators who
are about to decide the fate of an
important prisoner. (Mexico City,
replica in the National Museum
of Anthropology)

Below
The execution scene
Depiction of the sanguinary
Mayan rituals on the walls of the
second room of the palace of
Bonampak. In front of his assembled warriors, King Chan
Muan executes the captive chieftain, striking him with his spear,
while other prisoners, who have
been tortured, beg for mercy.
(Mexico City, replica in the National Museum of Anthropology)

Yaxchilán, on the Usumacinta
On the hills by the great river of Chiapas stand ruins that are gradually being cleared of the invading vegetation. The great Mayan site, on the frontier between Mexico and Guatemala, possesses Classic palaces whose style ressembles that of Palenque: mansard-style roofs, high openwork *cresterias*, wide stairways, etc. Structure 33, whose roof once bore various stucco sculptures, counts among the best preserved of the site.

Surrounded by the forest
On the steep banks of the Usumacinta, Structure 33 of Yaxchilán dominates the whole surrounding landscape at a height of 65 m. Known as the "Palace of the King", it contained a broken sculpture depicting "Bird-Jaguar", dating from 757.

Palaces with sculpted lintels
The originality of Yaxchilán lies in the wide stone lintels whose lower facet is richly sculpted; these replace the more usual beams of sapodilla wood. These works have resisted time's ravages better than the buildings themselves.

Pacal, the master of Palenque, won over "Shield-Jaguar". This event, which is only reported in Palenque sources (the Yaxchilán inscriptions maintain a discreet silence) underlines once again the endemic state of war that existed in Maya territory. In order to obtain sacrificial victims, the tribal chiefs had to confront their neighbours and capture prisoners, who were then put to death in triumphal celebrations. It is just such a "raid" that is narrated by the Bonampak frescoes (see below).

The ruler was a warrior chieftain, but, in Yaxchilán, this did not rule out political status for women. Lady Xok, the wife of "Shield-Jaguar", played the role of a true queen. On bas-reliefs, she is depicted presiding at ceremonies and taking part in grand rituals, and handing the king his war helmet as he set off on a campaign to secure captives for sacrifice to the gods.

The Monuments of Yaxchilán

The main buildings of the river city – the Usumacinta formed a territorial limit, since there is no construction on the opposite bank – present analogies with those of Palenque: similar dressed stone walls, mansard-style roofs and identical *cresterias*. As at Palenque, the crenellated roof combs atop the buildings of Yaxchilán supported stucco sculptures. Today, they have been so badly eroded by wind and vegetation that this is difficult to imagine.

The gigantic Temple 33, dominating the centre of the city, is the work of "Bird-Jaguar" and Lady Xok; it celebrates the lofty deeds of their reign. It contains a vast array of bas-reliefs, in which the rulers associate the heir apparent with the great ceremonies over which they presided in the middle of the eighth century.

Despite the ubiquitous forest, the city plan, carefully mapped by an American

The attentions of a wife
One of the most splendid sculpted lintels of Yaxchilán (no. 26), dating from 724, comes from Building 23. It shows, on the right, Dame Xok giving King Shield-Jaguar his war helmet. The power of the carving and the delicacy of the detail make this work one of the master-pieces of Classic sculpture. (Mexico City, National Museum of Anthropology)

Scene of court ritual
Lintel 53 of Yaxchilán, measuring 160 cm and dating from 766, shows a court scene: the sover-eign Bird-Jaguar, holding a figurine-septre in his right hand, receives homage from his wife. (Mexico City, National Museum of Anthropology)

Execution of a prisoner
Stela 15 from Yaxchilán dates from
A.D. 681, and shows Shield-Jaguar
preparing to sacrifice a prisoner
whom he holds by the hair. As in
the Bonampak mural, the king
executes his captive with a spear.
(Mexico City, National Museum of
Anthropology)

expedition, suggests that major terracing works must have taken place. The perimeters of the acropolises were remodelled, stairways climbed the hills and led to sanctuaries, pyramids stood atop hillocks – in short, the whole landscape was the stage of a veritable theatrical project which transformed nature into a grandiose ceremonial centre. The buildings cover the bank of the majestic river and stand one above the other on the rugged slopes, buried in tropical vegetation.

The evolution of vision

The vision of Palenque changed between the first explorations of Antonio Del Río, in 1787, whose drawings appeared in 1822, the more precise impressions of Friedrich Waldeck in 1832 for the book by Brasseur de Bourbourg published in 1865 and finally the impressions of Désiré Charnay, published in 1885. Thus, the famous tower of the Great Palace of Palenque is portrayed in differing ways. Similarly, in the depiction of the Throne of the Jaguars, a shallow-relief stucco carving from the Palace, the versions of Del Río, dating from 1787, then of Castañeda in 1805 for Captain Dupaix (published in 1835) and of Waldeck (1832) suggest a gradual evolution toward realism.

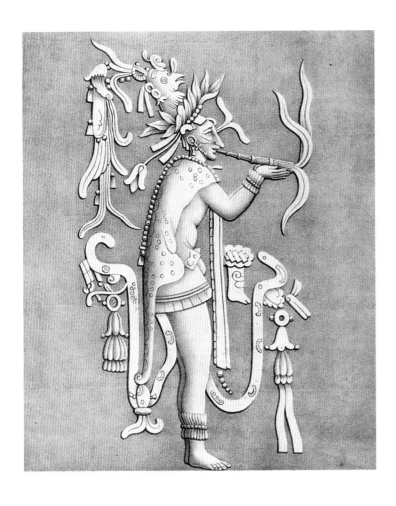

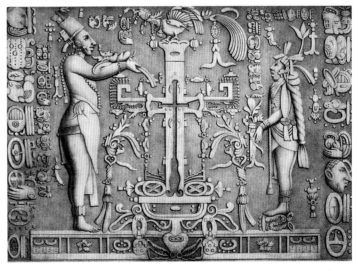

A relief in the Temple of the Cross at Palenque (dating from 690) showing a deity (God L) smoking a cigar, according to the Mayan custom that still exists today among the Lacandons, is recorded first by Castañeda in 1805 – who reversed the scene – then by Friedrich Waldeck in 1832 (right). In the depiction of the large sculpted panel at the back of the Temple of the Cross at Palenque, the image is similarly reversed in Castañeda's drawing for Dupaix, whereas the Waldeck drawing records the correct position, with King Chan Balum on the right and the Cosmic Tree surmounted by the Sky Bird in the centre and, lastly, Pacal on the left.

A Neglected Chapter of Maya Art

The Río Bec and Chenes Styles

Page 103

A monumental sculpture
This large seated figure (156 cm) in painted stucco from the southern zone of the Yucatán peninsula (Campeche or Quintana Roo) depicts a masked ruler carrying a war-axe and an emblematic shield. It probably dates from the sixth to seventh centuries. (Private Collection)

Situated between the Petén lowlands to the south and the scrubland of Yucatán to the north, the intermediate region covering the territories of Campeche and Quintana Roo is undoubtedly the most overlooked province of the Maya world. For the most part uninhabited today, these lands are covered in tropical forest, where palm trees and sapodillas mingle with dense vegetation. For a long time, only *chicleros*, prospecting for chewing-gum, frequented these parts and, in so doing, discovered a series of highly interesting Maya centres – for the style of the monuments hidden beneath the creepers and accumulations of humus is truly original.

These recently explored zones cover the south of the Yucatán, not far from the Guatemalan border. They lie in Mexican territory on either side of the road that links the modern town of Chetumal in the east, on the Caribbean sea, to the Escarcega in the west, between Campeche and Villahermosa. The main cities are Kohunlich, Dzibanché, Xpuhil, Becan and Chicanna.

The current efforts of Mexican archaeologists to protect, restore and render accessible the rediscovered monuments are helping to rectify a misconception widely held since the pioneering days of Maya exploration. Indeed, according to Sylvanus Morley, Maya chronology was divided into Old Empire (the Classic period in Guatemala and Honduras) and New Empire (the Postclassic period in the north of Yucatán).

This approach, inherited from Egyptology, is no longer valid. We know that certain Yucatán sites date from the Preclassic era and are not therefore later than their counterparts in the Petén. We also know that there was neither cultural exchange nor migration of population after the abandonment of the cities of Tikal, Copán and Palenque. The Maya at the end of the Classic era did not flee towards the capitals of the north in order to give a second wind to their declining civilization in the Postclassic period. No such explanation for the decline of the great cities can now be entertained.

Indeed, no other proof is needed of the error of the two major phases (Old and New Empire) theory than this intermediary zone which now presents itself as a narrow link between north and south, from both the geographical and historical points of view.

The Temple of Masks at Kohunlich

The Temple of Masks discovered on the site of Kohunlich, near Chetumal, dates from the dawn of the Classic period. On its western side, it features a series of large stucco faces which were originally polychrome. These masks are arranged in four layers on either side of a central stairway. The monumental decor is reminiscent of the temple of Cerros in Belize like the Preclassic building of Cerros, Kohunlich has a façade decorated with superb solar effigies. These intact reliefs were rediscovered under a later, decayed layer of stonework. The tradition of superposing one building onto another allows us to see examples of earlier architecture in a surprisingly good state of preservation.

A lord in ceremonial costume
On this Mayan stela from the Classic period, the ruler, wearing a deity mask headdress, decorated with large quetzal feathers, holds in his right hand a figurine-sceptre and in his left a ceremonial rod. Round his neck is a wide necklace composed of four rows of large jade beads. (Oaxaca, Rufino Tamayo Museum)

The solar theme illustrated by these large stylized stuccoes displays strongly cosmological themes. The prominence of this exuberant decoration is the outward expression of devotional practices related to astronomically based cults. Soon, however, rituals based on the movements of the heavens and the rhythms of the calendar merged with dynastic themes. These accompanied the rise in influence of those who held power. Veritable family trees, with "portrait galleries" of ancestors, were depicted, fusing their appearance with that of the sun. Such symbolism dictated the entire spatial organisation. For the temple was built in honour both of the gods who were worshipped there and of the rulers who represented them on earth by officiating in the sanctuaries.

Similar masks – now for the most part destroyed – have come to light during excavations on the site of Dzibanché, recently opened to the public. Here, as at Kohunlich, the structures that emerge from the forest conform to a strict scheme: acropolises, pyramids, esplanades, squares and platforms are organized on an orthogonal grid. They make it possible to read the often very elaborate urban plan of the various sectors of these districts. The palaces and ball courts alternate with sanctuaries. Also present are many earth basements that once supported private dwellings built of wood and palms.

Certain pyramids uncovered in Quintana Roo attain huge proportions. But these buildings are not related to those of Tikal, which feature tiny *cella* at the top of a very steep stepped base: here, even though the angle of the pyramid is acute, the sanctuary, far from being a tiny *cella*, spreads out widthwise and contains several half-collapsed vaulted chambers. This leads us to think that several priests were needed to conduct the rituals simultaneously.

A palace emerges from the forest
A great palace of Kohunlich displays its rooms at the top of a wide sweep of stairs. The building, which has just been restored, is constructed in regularly dressed stone and dates from the end of the Classic period.

From the top of the acropolis
Structure 3, recently cleared, exemplifies the damage caused by the rain forest to the buildings of Kohunlich.

Recently uncovered

On the vast site of Dzibanché (Campeche), the restoration works concentrate on pyramids of several levels that are traversed by a central stairway. This one leads to a high sanctuary and demonstrates the development of the temple in comparison with the tiny cells of the sanctuaries of Tikal.

Large solar effigy

Protected by later structures, this great stucco mask decorated the Pyramid of the Masks of Kohunlich. Traces of paint remain. These intact sculptures date from the beginning of the Classic period (around 500) and resemble the decoration of the pyramids at Uaxactún or Cerros.

The Fake Towers of Xpuhil

The giant pyramids of Tikal deeply marked the Maya imagination. Thus we find this theme transposed to emblematic mode in certain Río Bec and Chenes-style buildings of Quintana Roo: especially the three-tower structure that dominates the site of Xpuhil. Here, the extremely steep pyramidal "sanctuaries" are effectively inaccessible. The great stairways that climb the round-cornered towers are counterfeit: their steps are no longer wide enough to allow them to be climbed. The upper *cella* is solid all through, and its door is replaced by a huge mask of a celestial deity.

From this time on, Río Bec architecture – a name derived from the first known site – is nothing but decoration. It no longer had to convey a liturgical role and confined itself to a symbolic function, that of evoking the world of the gods. So, in a formalist system that had lost its original function, the sanctuaries came to have a purely semiological significance. The pyramid and its sanctuary were reduced to a type of commemorative monument. These "fake" towers are found not only in the Río Bec style but also, less frequently, in the Chenes style.

Buildings with Monsters' Jaws

Further west, on Campeche territory, the site of Chicanna – where restoration work is currently being carried out – contains a series of original structures. The term *chicanna* in Maya language means "house of serpent's fangs". The name refers to the best preserved building: no. II. This is a construction with a typical Chenes-style façade: the central section is transformed into a gigantic serpent's mouth in the image of the creator god Itzamna. The doorway reproduces the fearsome jaws – edged with enormous teeth modelled in sharp relief – above which the stylized eyes of the cosmic monster stare out.

This decor-cum-architecture, intended for some initiation rite peculiar to the peoples who lived in the late Classic period (between A.D. 550 and 700), is devised in schematic and symmetrical terms. The forms of the celestial deity are fashioned using a veritable puzzle of stone blocks all painstakingly carved. Assembled in sharp relief, the image imparts a sharply delineated profile and obsessive rhythm to the overall design the vertical sunlight of the Tropics shows this off to full advantage.

This gaping mouth – which has been likened to the mythical "cavern" depicted by the Olmecs in the altar of La Venta, where a cross-legged seated figure emerges from the jaws of the cosmic monster – finds a later transposition in the Quetzal-coatl-Kukulkan deity worshipped by the Toltec-Maya at Chichén Itzá.

Is this a colossal sculpture or an ornamental construction? The genius of the Maya from the area known as Chenes – the name of the neighbouring hills – is to have made "inhabitable sculptures" out of their temples – sanctuaries, that is, with a liturgical function, in which the rite of passage could be practised quite literally in spatial terms.

Structure II at Chicanna, with its three entrances each leading into two parallel

An exemplary restoration
In this detail of a structure of Dzibanché, the recent anastylosis carried out by the archaeologists contrasts, with great integrity, the ancient sections, which have retained their outer facing of smooth stone, with the projecting stones of the modern retaining walls (see the photograph on page 109).

Page 111
The main pyramid
At Dzibanché, several groups of pyramids form sacred complexes. The great four-storey pyramid that has recently been restored possesses a wide stairway that sweeps up the front to reach a largely preserved top sanctuary. Square and rounded platforms are superposed to form the levels that support the sanctuary.

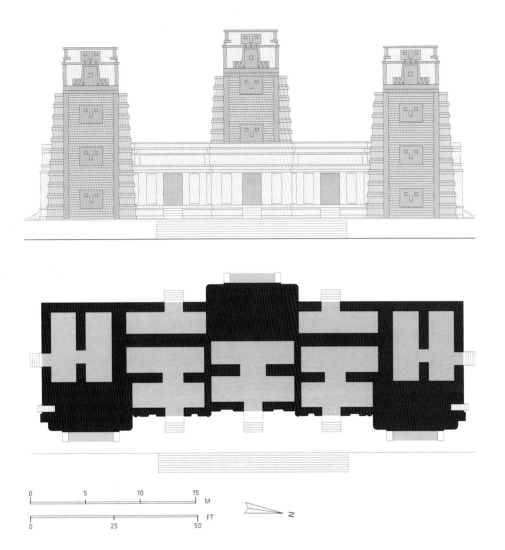

An illusory temple-palace
On the site of Xpuhil, the main building, in Río Bec style, is composed of three towers in a quincunx formation, between which are rooms arranged in pairs. The elevation shows that the towers are so steep that the stairs cannot be climbed.

rooms, one set behind the other, resembles a palace. However, it seems to have functioned not as a palace but a place of worship. Here, too, Chenes art plays on the barely perceptible distinction between one category and another. Temple and living quarters so resemble each other that it is not always possible to decide a building's function.

Other buildings at Chicanna – such as the recently restored Structure XX – depict the jaws of the cosmic porch of a pyramid. The entrance borrows, in simplified form, the motif of the doorway in the form of the jaws of a monster, ready to swallow up the spectator. Behind this dramatic entrance stands the pyramid, at whose summit two sanctuaries standing back to back were surmounted by a high *cresteria*.

There, the motif of the jaws of the celestial monster was repeated around the entrance to the *cella*-shaped rooms, through which the officiating priests had to pass in order to celebrate the rituals.

At the corners of this tower standing on top of Structure XX at Chicanna are rows of masks of the god Chac. This is a feature that one frequently finds in the Yucatán Puuc style. The schematic mask features a long, sinuous nose – which early visitors to Maya ruins sometimes mistook for a trumpet – and symmetrical features (eyes, eyebrows, ears etc.), which, curiously, bear a marked resemblance to the *t'ao t'ieh* masks of early Chinese bronzes.

Río Bec architecture

The monumental palace of Xpuhil, dating from the end of the Classic period (A.D. 700–800), is decorated with imitation sanctuaries and trompe-l'oeil façades at the top of its abrupt towers. The building nevertheless has considerable presence and great originality.

In the image of the gods

The decoration of the palace of Xpuhil is based on a series of quasi-abstract motifs, in which one nevertheless perceives the mask of the god, with its symmetrical eyes, ears and eyebrows and central nose and mouth.

Chicanna and the Chenes style
Structure XX of the site of Chicanna (Campeche) is a pyramid with a high two-level summit where the exuberant decoration of the Chenes style is given free rein. It is created by using a mosaic of elements to form a casing for the stonework.

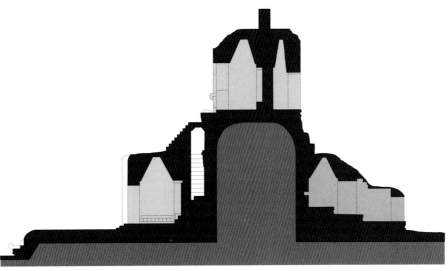

Section of Structure XX
The strange pyramidal construction of Chicanna supports a sanctuary that stands on top of a low, partially ruined temple.

Omnipresence of the god
The motifs that decorate the corners of Structure XX at Chicanna depict a recurrent image of the mask of Chac, god of rain. With his long nose in the form of a trunk, his spiral-shaped eyes and his jaws filled with curved fangs, Chac pervades the whole structure.

Plan of the site of Chicanna
Representative of the Chenes style, the Mayan site of Chicanna, in Campeche, is composed of several groups of buildings in the process of being cleared of vegetation and restored:
1. *Chultun*
2. Structure II
3. Structure III
4. Structure I
5. Structure IV
6. Structure IX
7. Structure VI
8. Structure XX

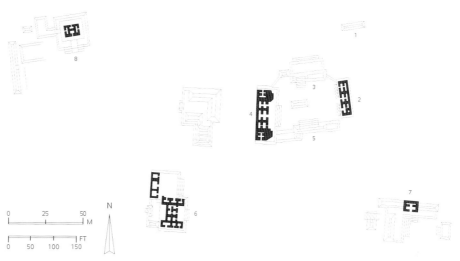

The square of Becan
Surrounded by public and religious buildings, the eastern *plaza* of the Mayan city of Becan, in Campeche, features a circular platform for human sacrifice.

Page 116
Like the huge jaws of a monster
The façade of Structure II at Chicanna is a typical example of the Chenes style: the building is transformed into sculpture. The central doorway assumes the form of the enormous jaws of the cosmic god Itzamna. Behind a row of fangs, the doorway itself seems to be part of the rite of passage (initiation). The spiral eyes and projecting nose of the monster, as well as the threshold edged with teeth, which plays the role of the lower jaw, together constitute the mask of the god. The image is created through sculpted blocks that form a vast mosaic of stone.

Becan – a Fortified City

Not far from Chicanna, in Campeche, the Maya site of Becan possesses a distinctive character which has been revealed by excavation: namely, a circular moat that forms a fortified ditch around the ceremonial centre. This moat was 9 m deep and enclosed an area of around 600 by 500 m: it was crossed by causeways. Situated on a sort of acropolis, the city contained several complexes including courtyards surrounded by pyramids.

The most impressive *plaza,* situated to the east, comprises four structures and is built on huge man-made platforms, with temples on three sides, the fourth being reserved for palace use. In the centre of the open space, a circular platform served the human sacrifices and sanguinary rituals of the Maya tribes.

Heading northwards, we come to another lower court which is surrounded by several structures. These include huge pyramidal masses that have yet to be explored. A corbelled arch leads to a ball court surrounded by various buildings. To the west, a complex of pyramids stands close by a series of courtyards. These would seem to have contained housing made of perishable materials. Together the pyramid complex and residential courtyards form the western limit of the city's ceremonial centre.

It seems that Becan acquired its fortifications between A.D. 200 and 600, right in the middle of the Classic period. It was, however, only at the end of the Classic period, between 600 and 850, that the city was endowed with the majority of the buildings visible today, under which earlier structures doubtless lie dormant. But Becan's life as a city did not end with the Classic period; it enjoyed a last creative surge between 900 and 1200. The explanation is probably the arrival from the high Mexican plateaus of contingents of foreigners who influenced Becan's culture as they did that of Chichén Itzá.

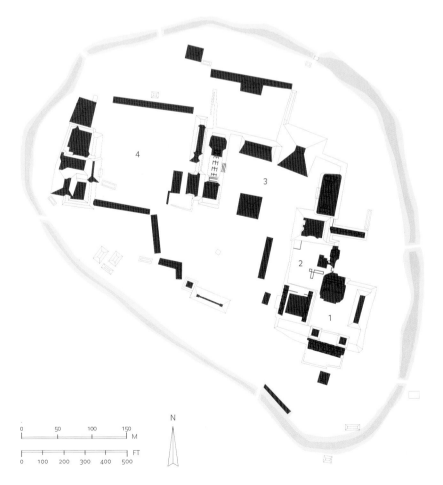

The restored ball court
In the centre of the city of Becan, the two banks of the ball court lie next to the western *plaza*. They are slightly sloping, as at Copán.

A city surrounded by a moat
A moat surrounds twenty hectares that form the ceremonial centre of Becan, whose squares are in the process of being restored:
1. The eastern *plaza*
2. The intermediary terrace
3. The central square with its pyramid
4. The western *plaza*

Cleared of vegetation
Structure IV of Becan, now cleared of vegetation, is a wide pyramid with vast "apartments" situated 18 m up. Its proud bulk dominates the eastern *plaza*.

The Palace-Temple of Edzná

Before leaving the Campeche region, we should also mention a complicated building constructed at Edzná, in the north-west of the state: the five-storey Pyramid-Temple. Once again, we are faced with a building that combines in typical Río Bec style two different types of construction. On the one hand, we have a pyramid, surmounted by its upper sanctuary, access to which is through a large uninterrupted central stairway. The *cella* is surmounted by a high *cresteria*, reaching a height of 31 m. On the other hand, we have a palace, whose four superposed levels, each slightly set back above the other, contain various chambers reached through the doors that punctuate the façade. On the lowest and highest levels, these rooms are preceded by porticoes. On the lowest level, these are constructed with shafts made of masonry, whereas the higher level possesses monolithic columns, which resemble those of the Yucatán Puuc style.

The edifice at Edzná is built on a square ground plan, 58 by 60 m. A pyramidal structure, it dominates a courtyard 160 by 148 m formed by an artificial esplanade that raises the courtyard level by 6 m. A stairway, 45 m wide, flanks this raised area, which is bordered on either side by devotional buildings, following a design that is an example of the generous sense of proportions possessed by this Maya people between the seventh and eighth centuries.

The site also contains a series of stelae covering the period from 672 to 810, whereas the steps of the large stairway climbing the pyramid bear glyphs going back to 652.

Finally, the city of Edzná was linked to the sea by a man-made canal 12 km long, with a gradient not exceeding 0.5 m every 1000 m. With the help of the Río Champoton, this made it possible for canoes to carry on a flourishing trade with the coast of the Gulf of Mexico and the cities of Yucatán.

The man-made terrace
Seen from the summit of the main pyramid, the man-made terrace of Edzná, in Campeche, is surrounded by religious buildings that overlook a central platform intended for sacrifices.

The five-storey pyramid at Edzná
Combining the principle of the pyramid and the multi-level palace, the acropolis of Edzná is a huge creation, on a square plan, 60 m long on each side. The five levels, surmounted by the *cresteria* of the sanctuary, are linked by a single central flight of steps. Each level contains rooms, with those on the bottom level preceded by pairs of masonry columns.

A orthogonal arrangement
The main pyramid of Edzná stands within a huge general scheme conceived for the most part in the eighth century and covering around 2.5 hectares.

A lookout over the scrubland
As in the Chenes region – which, like Edzná, marks the transition toward the Puuc zone – the rectangular pyramids possess vast oblong chambers. The man-made acropolis elevates the buildings above the forest plain of the Yucatán peninsula.

The Maya Cosmos and Deities

To attempt to define the cosmology and the Maya Pantheon in a few lines is something of a challenge. The world of the pre-Columbians was peopled with deities and forces that had to be ceaselessly placated with sacrifices and offerings – in particular with human blood. Whoever did not conform to this ritual risked incurring divine wrath or breaking the cosmic cycles.

The Maya universe was organized on a vertical axis resembling a tree uniting nadir and zenith. It was the axis of a world situated between the god Itzamna, monster of the universe, and the goddess Ixchel, symbol of the moon. The axis was surmounted by the divine bird, or Bird-Serpent. The celestial vault is supported by four divinities: the Bacabs. The earth was organized on an orthogonal framework, where the points of the compass were represented by colours: red Chac denotes the East; white Chac the North; black Chac the West; and yellow Chac the South.

The gods are so numerous that specialists have designated them by letters of the alphabet: god A represents death; B is long-nosed Chac, god of rain and thunder; god L and god N reign over Xibalba, the Afterlife; god M rules over war and traders; god Q presides at sacrifices wearing the zero sign, a symbol of death. The planets too (Venus as Morning and as Evening Star), have their divine symbols. They played a crucial role in forecasting the future. The Sun itself is represented by the great Jaguar. Each astral god has different characteristics according to whether it is in the ascendant or descendant part of its cycle.

All the gods could adopt traits belonging to other deities and form composite beings. It is the way in which they accumulate attributes from different sources that makes Maya mythology so complex.

A clergy and specific rituals were assigned to each deity honoured in a city, and its tale is told by the great myths. We find echoes in a late text: the *Popol Vuh*, the sacred book of the Quichés of the south of Guatemala, which was written down in the middle of the sixteenth century. The book of *Chilam Balam*, also transcribed during the colonial period, describes prophecies. The attempt to predict the future, particularly through astrology, was essential to the Maya world.

THE PUUC STYLE IN YUCATÁN

The Splendour of Uxmal's Palaces

Page 125
The mask of the god Chac
The image of the rain god is present everywhere on the front of Puuc-style buildings in Yucatán. Created by means of a mosaic composed of carefully carved stone blocks in a recurring pattern, the masks form an intricate assemblage on the friezes of temples and palaces.

In the jaws of the serpent
This sculpture that projected from the front of the Pyramid of the Magician at Uxmal (Yucatán) represents a human face emerging from the open jaws of the cosmic serpent. Here, we have a motif that originated in the northern Mexican plateaux, based on the mythical plumed serpent. (Mexico City, National Museum of Anthropology)

The vast flat region of Yucatán, a peninsula between the Caribbean sea and the Gulf of Mexico, is mainly known for its fine archaeological sites rich in Puuc-style monuments. In terms of monumental architecture, the style that developed at Uxmal, Kabah, Labna, Sayil, Xlapak or Chacmultún represents the golden age for Maya cities of the eighth and ninth centuries A.D. In this region, the destructive power of the vegetation was never as fierce as in the Petén. The buildings discovered in these scrublands have not suffered the same ravages as those situated in the tropical forest of Guatemala and Quintana Roo.

The Dzibilchaltún Excavations

The first structures to appear in the Yucatán region go far back into the past. Certain Preclassic remains date from the fifth century B.C. Where the Classic period is concerned, archaeologists discovered on the site of Acanceh a pyramid decorated with stucco masks – which have since disappeared. This sanctuary would seem to date from the fourth century A.D. and resembles those of Cerros and Uaxactún. Like the latter, the platform of Acanceh is built on a square ground plan, with four central stairways leading to an upper level that was surmounted by a *cella* built of daub and covered in thatch.

The formula of a quadruple stairway ascending all four sides of a pyramid recurs at Dzibilchaltún, where American archaeologists uncovered a very unusual sanctuary. It lay beneath the ruined superstructure of a later building that had hidden it from view at the end of the Classic period. Named the Temple of the Seven Dolls (Structure I or *Templo de los Siete Muñecas*), this ancient pyramid is thought to date from around A.D. 450, though this remains controversial.

At the top of the pyramid stands a stone building with a central doorway on all four sides, surmounted by a decorative frieze. At the corners, "frameworks" of salient stone are all that remain of the stucco masks depicting Chac, god of rain; he was particularly revered in the north of Yucatán, where rain was often scarce. In the centre of the flat stonework roof stood a square-based tower which played the role of a three-dimensional *cresteria*. Its massive bulk emphasizes the double axial symmetry of the sanctuary.

Inside this lofty temple, a corbel-vaulted gallery runs around the central core. In addition to the four doors leading into it, there are two windows open to the outside which let light into the gallery. This formula of openings that do not extend right down to the ground is original to the Maya region. It was, however, applied only in a few Puuc-style buildings.

The Temple of the Seven Dolls of Dzibilchaltún, which has been remarkably well restored, is evidence that a sophisticated architectural style existed in the north of Yucatán from the middle Classic period. Thus, from the first, tentative constructions of the first millennium B.C. to the first buildings of Acanceh and of Dzibilchaltún, we can see the development of a style of stone architecture that was continuously refined until the eighth century A.D.

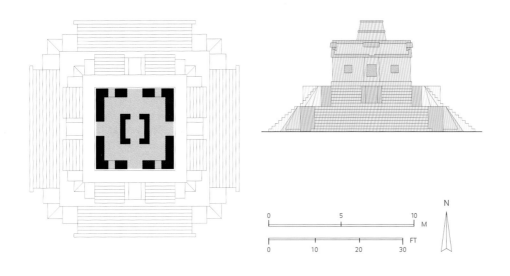

A structure on a square plan
Plan and elevation of the
temple of Dzibilchaltún, with
its orthogonal structure and
its vaulted passageway.

Hallmarks of Puuc Architecture

These beginnings were nevertheless rather humble, compared with the truly exceptional work produced in the north-west of Yucatán during the apogee of Puuc
art in the late Classic era. Maya architecture was to flourish over an area covering approximately 65 km from north to south and from east to west (some 4 000 km²). In
addition to the quality of the buildings, we should highlight elaborate town-planning schemes that characterized this period. The buildings are placed in a
series of complexes. Major palaces – low horizontal structures containing dozens of
rooms – contrast with pyramids and, most importantly, combine to form vast quadrangles. These are generally set on artificial platforms wholly created by hand.

Whether they were isolated palaces or quadrangles forming *plazas* or *patios*,
all the buildings designed for occupation by the ruling "caste" essentially stemmed

An archaic temple in Yucatán
On a square platform, accessible by
four central stairways, the Temple
of the Seven Dolls of Dzibilchaltún
has a strange configuration: the
door is flanked by windows, the
frieze displays the support-struc-
ture of the motifs that were once
covered by the stucco decoration,
and on the roof stands a structure
in the shape of a chimney – a
transformation of the traditional
cresteria.

Corbelled vaults
The corridor surrounding the *cella* of the temple of Dzibilchaltún is created by means of an elementary Mayan corbel vault. The square window is unusual in Yucatec architecture.

The capital of Puuc style
Plan of the city of Uxmal, with its various groups in the form of quadrangles:
1. Northern group
2. Cemetery group
3. Nunnery Quadrangle
4. Pyramid of the Magician
5. Ball court
6. House of the Turtles
7. Palace of the Governor
8. Great Pyramid
9. Pigeon Quadrangle
10. Southwestern group

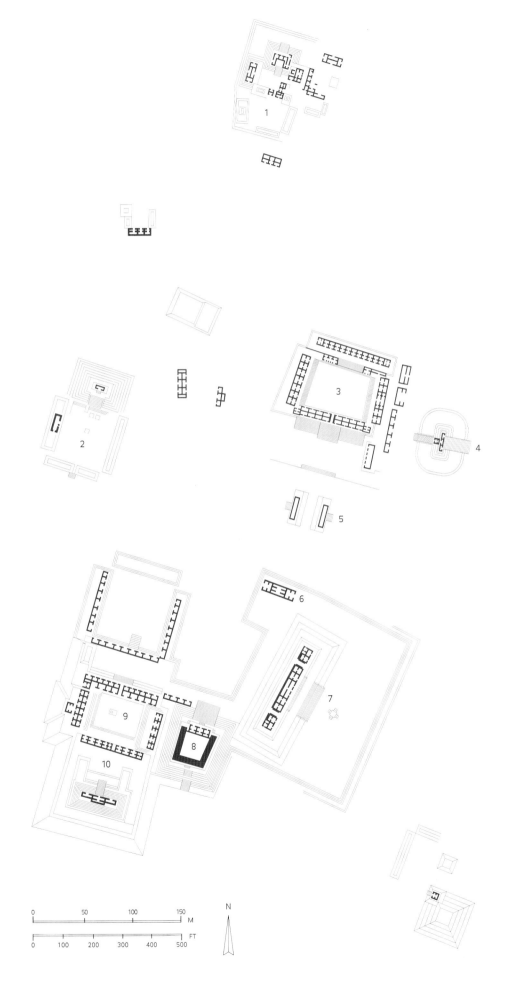

from a single principle. The rooms that they constituted were in effect simply huts constructed in stone rather than wattle and daub. This fact is amply demonstrated by the carvings of traditional thatch-roofed dwellings that are found above the doors of certain buildings.

Indeed, as was underlined at the beginning of this study, the concrete vaulted chamber represented the dwelling space and was the translation into stone of the inner area of the traditional hut. In this way, vernacular architecture influenced the construction schemes of the very largest palatial edifices built for the sovereign and his "nobles" – whether priests or warriors.

And two points arise from its architectural symbolism. On the one hand, this continuity between the hut and the palace demonstrates the extreme cohesion of Maya society, regardless of its hierarchical order. On the other, the outward appearance of "official" buildings, differed quite markedly from that of ordinary dwellings. On the façade, the stone frieze, abundantly decorated with relief sculptures, contributed to the grandiose appearance of these buildings. In this way, Mayan relief art served architecturally to exalt the ruling class, whose residences, overlaid with a sumptuous veneer, proclaimed their absolute power.

But this ornamentation was invariably linked to traditional sources. In addition to the hut-like configuration mentioned, we should note the criss-cross motif of wattlework and the grid-like surfaces, produced by the working of wood. This also applies to the rows of baluster-like logs above the entrances and to shapes whose outline is simply a transposition of the ties and the straw wadding of the common dwelling.

The arrangement of the buildings
General view of Uxmal seen from the top of the Pyramid of the Magician towards the south-west: on the left, a view onto the Palace of the Governor; in the centre, the stairs of the Great Pyramid; on the right in the foreground, the House of the Turtles, and further back, the Pigeon Quadrangle, crowned with motifs in the form of *cresterias*.

On the Yucatec plain
The whole of Uxmal, seen from the terrace of the Palace of the Governor, looking north-east: on the left, the side of the House of the Turtles; in the centre, the ball court in front of the Nunnery Quadrangle with, on the right, the Pyramid of the Magician.

The Apotheosis of Uxmal

Like pivotal points dominating the site, the great pyramids of Uxmal – in particular the Pyramid of the Magician – form a contrast with the long spectacular façades of the palaces, whose friezes, decorated with recurrent motifs and subtle rhythmical designs, are set off by the unchanging skyline of Yucatán. As early as the sixteenth century, Bishop Diego de Landa wrote that the region owed its reputation to the profusion, grandeur and beauty of its Maya monuments.

The Pyramid of the Magician overlooks the Nunnery (it should be pointed out that these names hail from the imagination of the first visitors, the Spanish *conquistadores* who arrived in a country where the advanced Maya civilization had already started to wane three centuries earlier). It forms a truncated cone with rounded corners and has two stairways: the very steep one, to the west, is lined with effigies of the god Chac; the wider eastern stairway leads to the sanctuary of the upper platform (Temple IV) consisting of three adjoining rooms, whose roof stands 45 m above ground level.

This building is the outcome of a series of additions and alterations. Thus, the eastern stairway covers another more ancient one (the principle of superpositions), that led to a lower sanctuary (Temple II). At the base of the western side of the pyramid, archaeologists have discovered an earlier structure (Temple I) dating back to 569, according to carbon dating. The stairway flanked by masks leads to a higher sanctuary (Temple III) built in the Chenes style. Facing west, the sanctuary presents the gaping jaws of the Cosmic Serpent in the image of Itzamna, god of the sky. The influence of the art of Campeche and of Quintana Roo, discernible in the heart of Yucatán country, reveals the close links that the Maya tribes had forged amongst themselves.

From the high platform, the eye surveys the Nunnery Quadrangle. Its four palaces form a trapezoidal ground plan. Approaching from the south, the visitor climbs a wide sweep of steps measuring 80 m across, that lead to the southern palace, where eight doorways lead into various chambers. In the middle of the façade, a large arch – a veritable triumphal arch – forms the entrance to the *patio,* that is surrounded by three other buildings. Measured from façade to façade the courtyard is 85 m wide and 65 m deep.

In addition, the gradations of height around this huge space are carefully composed. Thus, the first stairway that leads to the monumental arch negotiates in a change of level of 4 to 5 m. At this level, the *patio* forms a vast flat area. It is flanked, to east and west alike, by flights of stairs that raise the lateral palaces by another 2 m. At the end, another stairway leads – between two protruding structures – to the terrace where the fourth palace stands 4 to 5 m higher up. The whole thus has an ascending scale. This interplay of multi-level volumes helps to enliven the spatial organization. Moreover, given the trapezoidal shape of the ground plan, the lack of orthogonality between the buildings has the effect of accelerating the perspective towards the narrower back of the courtyard.

The four palaces measure 85 m to the south, 50 m to the east, 55 m to the west and 85 m to the north; they do not meet at the corners, so the quadrangle is open. Visually, this lightens the whole composition and demonstrates a remarkable mastery of the handling of volume and mass.

The palaces of the Nunnery contain two rows of chambers providing fifty dwellings, plus a vast "ceremonial" apartment of six rooms in the middle of the eastern building.

An identical formula, that of four palaces around a *patio,* is found in the Pigeon Quadrangle, close to the Great Pyramid, in the south-western group. The same features – triumphal arch, buildings not quite joining at the corners – appear in this

The Pyramid of the Magician
In front of its rounded forms, the western side of the Pyramid of the Magician at Uxmal displays a great stairway lined with masks of Chac. It leads to the sanctuary with its Chenes-style façade, then to the upper temple, whose vast *cella* is in the usual Campeche style.

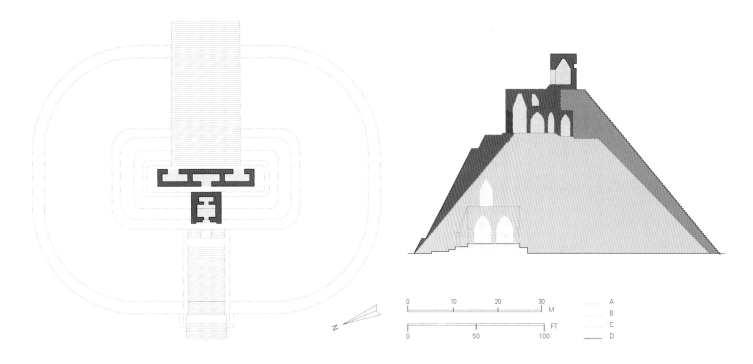

0   10   20   30
M

0   50   100
FT

A
B
C
D

Steps towards the sky

On its eastern side, the Pyramid of the Magician at Uxmal is dominated by the single flight of wide steps that sweeps without interruption from ground level to the upper platform.

Successive stages of construction

The plan and section of the Pyramid of the Magician at Uxmal reveal a succession of superposed sanctuaries, that mark the successive stages of the additions.

A Temple I
B Temple II
C Temple III
D Temple IV

The influence of the Chenes style
The entrance to the western sanctuary of the Pyramid of the Magician is surrounded by a Chenes-style façade. It reproduces the stylized image of the jaws of the cosmic monster.

The obsessive image of Chac
With his long nose in the form of an upturned trunk, his spiral eyes and eyebrows, the god of rain appears everywhere at Uxmal, particularly notable are those flanking the western stairs of the Pyramid of the Magician.

Page 135
A true ladder towards the gods
The vertiginous western stairs of the Pyramid of the Magician at Uxmal lead to the Chenes-style sanctuary. The volume of this steep construction is lightened by a transversal corbel-vaulted corridor built into its base.

group, itself preceded to the north by a complex that consists of three stone build-ings, with a single row of chambers. The platform that delimits the northern side is not surmounted by a palace: was this an unfinished project or a solution involving non-permanent structures?

Whatever the case, the style of town-planning typified by square areas is markedly present in the city of Uxmal, where there are several groups of this type. It bespeaks an intense tribal life and a concern for collective living-conditions gov-erned by real socio-political cohesion. It also shows that the stone-built city – be-longing to lofty politico-religious circles – with its complexes including a pyramid and a quadrangle, offers similarities to the medieval monasteries of the Christian world. Like the latter, with their church and cloister where members of the intelli-gentsia congregated, the "districts" of Maya cities formed cultural focal points. Perhaps these urban centres corresponded to various religious "orders", dedicated to the worship of the principal gods. Unfortunately, the extreme scarcity of in-scriptions makes it impossible to confirm any such hypothesis. It is, however, sup-ported by the names first given at the time of the Spanish conquest to the buildings even today known as the "Convent" or the "Nunnery".

The Ball Court

At the lowest point of the city, a ball court forms the link between the Nunnery and the imposing building called the Palace of the Governor, dominating Uxmal with its huge bulk. The two raised banks running along the area reserved for the teams once supported buildings where the elite members of the audience followed the vicissitudes of the ritual contest, which often culminated in human sacrifice.

Inscriptions have been found here during archaeological excavations. One of

A complex of buildings
The Nunnery Quadrangle at Uxmal, seen from the top of the Pyramid of the Magician: leaving the corners of the quadrangle open, the four great Puuc-style palaces are organized around a *patio*.

Asymmetry within symmetry
The façade of the northern palace of the Nunnery Quadrangle, 85 m wide, stands on a platform with a stairway flanked on either side by asymmetrical galleries.

A subtle arrangement
Elevation of the northern palace and plan of the Nunnery Quadrangle at Uxmal. The arrangement follows a trapezoid ground plan that rejects orthogonality:
1. Vaulted entrance
2. Southern Palace
3. Western Palace
4. Eastern Palace
5. Northern Palace

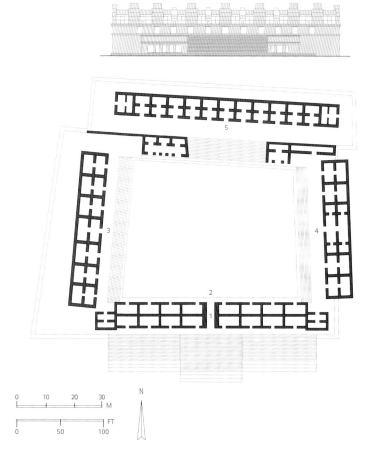

A rythmic, symbolic decorative scheme
The motifs that decorate the frieze of the eastern palace, overlooking the Nunnery Quadrangle at Uxmal, are based on an emblematic symbol of power: the ceremonial sceptres. In the centre of each motif appears a stylized head possibly depicting a sovereign.

View of the eastern palace
The frieze that runs above the doorways of the rooms is punctuated by a series of superposed ceremonial sceptres with a jaguar's head at each end. This decorative scheme stands out against a lattice-work background. The lower part of the façade uses double mouldings separated by short balusters.

The expressionism of the decorative scheme
The ends of the ceremonial sceptres decorating the friezes sometimes show jaguars, sometimes snakes equipped with powerful venomous fangs. This expresses the apotropaic protective function of the door.

View of the western palace
The frieze of the western building of the Nunnery Quadrangle is the result of a rearrangement: in its first state, it was composed of masks of Chac and of key patterns that stood out against an openwork background; then, under Mexican influence, the plumed serpent motif was superposed.

Page 140 above left

The image of Kukulkan
Decorating the western palace, the plumed serpent simultaneously displays its rattle tail and its jaws in which appears the human image of Quetzalcoatl, known as Kukulkan in Yucatan, the god of the Morning Star, symbol of resurrection.

Page 140 above right

The presence of Chac
At the corner of the eastern palace of the Nunnery Quadrangle of Uxmal, the stylized mask of Chac, god of rain, stands watch. Here, he has lost his trunk-shaped nose.

Page 140 below left

Guardian deities
At the four corners of the Puuc-style palace, as in Campeche, the superposed images of Chac stand guard as if to protect the dignitaries of the Mayan city.

Page 140 below right

The raised "trunk"
At Uxmal, the image of Chac, with its curved nasal appendage – which the first European visitors took to be the trunk of elephant! – is treated in a schematic way.

A triumphal entrance arch
The entrance to the Nunnery Quadrangle possesses a fine Mayan corbel-vaulted arch, created by means of a permanent stone casing into which the rubblework cement was poured.

them refers to the year 649, which is probably the date of this sports arena. In addition, a goal post found *in situ* refers to 901, a date at the very end of the Late Classic period. This chronological indication probably relates to the transformations made to the decoration of the building while Mexican influence on the Yucatán region was being felt. In this period, a sculpted torus (a convex moulding) representing the body of the Plumed Serpent – the Kukulkán of Chichén Itzá, or the Quetzalcoatl of Tula – was incorporated into the decoration of the building. This immense stone serpent coils around the inner walls of the sports court.

At the same time, the Maya embellished the façade of the western palace of the Nunnery with another representation of the great reptile that spreads its coils over the openwork motifs of the frieze. This Plumed Serpent, an enduring legend of the Toltec-Maya world, is identifiable by its rattlesnake's tail, covered in horny plates that produce loud vibrating sounds terrifying animals and people alike. From its gaping jaws there emerges the face of Man, a symbol of the resurrection incarnated in the dual planet Venus: Evening and Morning Star. Thus the ritual of life and death that finds concrete expression on the ball court lends Uxmal the deep sacred meaning of which its architecture is the perfect symbol.

The Palace of the Governor

The Palace of the Governor was so named by Fra Lopez de Cogolludo in his memoir published in 1688. He described it as the residence of the Maya rulers. The huge symmetrical façade, almost 100 m long, is made up of three sections: a central building 55 m long, and two wings, each 15 m long, which are linked to the main block by means of large corbelled archways with a span of 7 m. These were originally open

The ball court of Uxmal
In the centre of the great Puuc city, the area constructed for the ritual ball game consists of low banks and a lateral wall with stone rings through which the gum ball had to pass. The 649 building was modified in 901.

The Pigeon Quadrangle in Uxmal
The court known as the Pigeon Quadrangle, at Uxmal, is surmounted by a series of openwork tympanums in the form of *cresterias*. These unusual structures probably supported of sculpted decoration.

The Great Pyramid of Uxmal
A wide flight of steps leads to the single doorway of the upper sanctuary at the summit of the Great Pyramid of Uxmal. The neighbouring Pigeon Quadrangle is visible at the right.

The majestic royal façade

The three blocks that form the Palace of the Governor at Uxmal display their handsome façade at the top of a platform scaled by a monumental stairway. Almost 100 m, the building, with its two side-long wings linked by arches, possesses a frieze whose extended rythmic patterns counterpoints the eleven openings in the frontage.

A vast interior

Composed of the equivalent of three "apartments", the chamber that occupies the centre of the Palace of the Governor is a large assembly room, lit by three bays and boasting a splendid Mayan corbelled vault.

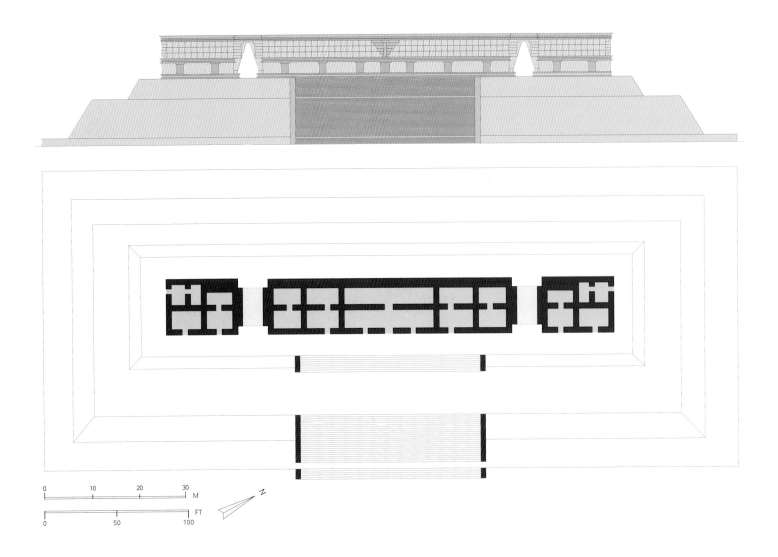

passageways between the buildings. During a second phase of building, they were filled in and adorned with columns forming symmetrical porticoes.

At the beginning of this study, we stressed the fact that certain Maya buildings stand on huge man-made substructures. The Palace of the Governor is a spectacular example. It stands on a first platform measuring 188 by 170 m, and 1.25 m high (30 000 m³); the second one, partially covering the first, measures 162 by 135 m and is 7.5 m in height (164 000 m³); a third base, scaled by a great stairway, measures 130 by 50 m and raises the palace by 6.3 m (40 000 m³). A last bank, 110 m long, 22 m wide and 3 m high (7 000 m³) serves as the base for the whole structure. These four superposed man-made esplanades, whose total height reaches 18 m, amount to 250 000 m³, or 450 to 500 000 tons of materials.

On this impressive basement, forming a sort of artificial acropolis, stands the resplendent façade of the Palace of the Governor, whose harmony, balance and obvious purity immediately strike all onlookers.

A closer study of this façade reveals its subtle rhythms: the central structure has seven doorways, whose symmetrical arrangement makes good use of irregular but repeated gaps. The wings each have two doors with an additional door on each end of the building.

To discover the "rhythm" that governs the arrangement of the openings punctuating the façade of the Palace of the Governor, we measured the length of wall separating one door from another. The result of this proceeding was a remarkable discovery: the Maya used only two dimensions: widths A and B. These may occur in single or double form (i.e. A and AA, B and BB). For the organization of the façade of the Palace of the Governor, we find the following symmetrical formulation:

A grandiose palace
Elevation and plan of the Palace of the Governor at Uxmal: composed of three blocks dominating the Yucatec plain, the building was the centre of power and was used for the court rituals of the Mayan princes.

A AA A – B BB AA B B AA BB B – A AA A

The solution is simple and subtle. It avoids monotony, while creating a close link between the wings and the central body of the building. If this rhythm is translated into metric dimensions, the result is roughly as follows:

3   6   3   –   3.5   7   6   3.5 3.5   6   7   3.5   –   3   6   3

These openings lead to 20 vaulted chambers – some are small and do not exceed 4 x 2.5 m, whereas others occupying the centre of the palace form fairly large reception rooms of up to 20 m by 4 m in width, permitting the staging of court rituals with an elaborate ceremonial.

Above these doors runs a huge stone mosaic frieze framed by two projecting cornices that form the top and central mouldings. On this ornamental surface almost 4 m high, which runs around the entire circumference of the palace and amounts to almost 1 000 m^2 of decoration, there are various elements: 1. high relief statuary, in particular in the large central motif; 2. masks of the god Chac at the corners of the construction and distributed in great wave-like patterns over the frieze; 3. stepped frets, solar symbols that also form a pattern distributed in waves over the whole surface of the frieze; 4. a network of pierced slabs reproducing the criss-cross pattern of "petrified" wickerwork. These repetitive features lead to the conclusion that Maya builders had their very own remarkably advanced production techniques (see below).

This decoration has huge symbolic significance. The distribution of motifs is organized around the central theme, where we see the sculpted effigy of the sovereign set against a background that consists of a series of superposed "ceremonial rods", in the form of cosmic serpents, a characteristic symbol of power in

To the glory of the sovereign
The decorative scheme in the middle of the frieze that runs around the Palace of the Governor at Uxmal is explicit: interrupting the rhythm of the key patterns and set above the door placed in the centre of the building, the statue of the king is seated on a throne. Above is a huge crown of quetzal feathers. The motif stands out against the horizontal ceremonial sceptres whose extremities are decorated with the jaws of stylized jaguars.

An austere design
In contrast with the exuberance of the frieze, the design of the short balusters underlining the base of the building imparts a formal rigour to the Palace of the Governor at Uxmal.

Mayan cities. In this way, the repetitive motifs were centered around the figure of the king. They associate the masks of Chac, god of rain, with the frets representing the Sun. Sun and Rain are the driving forces behind any agrarian society. Here we are in the presence of the forces of nature in a world governed by the climatic rhythms on which agriculture depends. These themes are clearly visible on the lattice work inspired by the primitive hut, as if to link the whole Amerindian population with the hierarchy of power culminating in the person of the ruler himself.

Page 149
An arch at the Palace of the Governor
At the edge of the southern wing of the Palace of the Governor at Uxmal, a Mayan arch with a concave intrados originally formed an open bay. Subsequently, this bay was closed up by a dividing wall and ornamented with a columned portico. Parts of the columns have survived (in the foreground).

Balusters and turtles
A detail from the sober decoration of the Turtle House at Uxmal dating, like the Palace of the Governor, from the late ninth century.

Balance and harmony
The side façade of the Turtle House, standing by the Palace of the Governor, possesses an admirable simplicity: between two bands, a row of cylindrical balusters forms the frieze above the two small and one large doors.

Mass Production and the Division of Labour

The mask of the god Chac
A schematic effigy of Chac is formed of stereotyped elements – eyes, ears, jaws and long nose. The visage of the god of rain is thus repeated *ad infinitum* on the friezes of Puuc-style palaces.

Superposition of gods
At the corners of the Palace of the Governor, a series of Chac masks are stacked, one above the other, as if to mount guard over the ruler. These repetitive motifs were produced in great numbers by the Maya.

First, a calculation: the mosaic frieze decorating the Palace of the Governor at Uxmal encircles the whole edifice, which is 100 m long and 15 m wide; the total length of the frieze is therefore 230 m. The ornamentation forms a band a little less than 4 m in height. Its area, as we have seen, is 1 000 m^2. A detailed examination shows that this decoration is made up of 230 masks of Chac, 106 frets and some 300 m^2 of stone lattice work.

Each mask of Chac measuring 1.2 by 0.6 m is composed of nineteen blocks forming a symmetrical structure: one block for the nose in the form of a "trump", four similar blocks for the ears, two pairs of two blocks for the ornaments situated on and under the ears, two blocks for the eyes, two blocks for the eyebrows, two blocks for the cheeks, and two blocks for the jaw. There are thus 460 identical blocks for the eyes, 920 similar blocks for the ears and so on.

As regards the pierced areas covering almost 300 m^2 of frieze, they are formed from square elements decorated with a St. Andrew's cross measuring 20 cm across (or 25 elements to the m^2). The builders therefore needed 6 000 identical blocks in all. Within the strict framework of the frieze, the slightest difference of one or two centimetres could therefore disrupt the general organization of the repeated motif. One can appreciate that this work required flawless precision and technical skill.

What is implied by this combination of technical mastery and the manufacture of many identical elements? This type of production was certainly based on marked specialization, and on a division of labour into several teams, each working on a particular motif and intervening at a precise stage. There was a distinction between coarse stone cutting in the quarry, sawing into basic units, rough hewing of the stone and finally the carving of the blocks by teams of workers who had clearly differentiated skills. In particular, the sculptors responsible for the finishing touches must have been accomplished craftsmen.

Work of this kind indicates the existence of a fully-fledged system of mass production. This is a concept that stems from industrial methods and it comes as something of a surprise in a world just emerging from the Neolithic period. It is a startling thing to find in a civilization that had neither metallurgy nor mechanical technology at its disposal. But, as with hieroglyphic writing, positional and vigesimal mathematics and the astronomical calendar, it exemplifies the advances that Maya society had achieved in certain fields.

THE DIVERSITY OF THE YUCATEC CITIES

Palaces, Arches and Observatories

Page 153
Image of a Yucatec chief
Shallow relief carving is rare in the Puuc-style region: those that have been recently discovered at Kabah (Yucatán) adorn the doorjambs. They represent armed chieftains or kings, wearing the apparel of high-ranking dignitaries.

The "King of Kabah"
This scupture fragment, known for several decades, shows a moustachioed figure, marked with ritual scarring and wearing a crown. It comes from the same group as the full-length statues recently uncovered on the site of Kabah, that one can admire *in situ* (see page 160). Its expressionist style demonstrates an aesthetic far removed from the art of Palenque. (Mexico City, National Museum of Anthropology)

The great majority of buildings dating from the eighth and ninth centuries in the Maya cities of Yucatán are in the Puuc style of architecture. The towns of Kabah, Sayil, Labna, Xlapak or Chacmultún form a veritable constellation of monuments south of Uxmal, which was the probable capital of the Yucatec rulers.

One of the richest founts of information is Kabah itself, whose palaces have been the object of recent excavations and restorations. The Codz Poop, or Palace of the Masks, the most remarkable building at the site, presents a façade entirely covered with masks of the god Chac. These stone masks are all identical. They stand one on top of the other from the base to the top cornice and run in rows over the whole length of the building, from which stone hooks protrude to form the nose of the deity. Thus the palace has no less than 260 effigies of the god of rain. This accumulation reflects an obsessive litany based on unchanging repetition, from which it draws its spell-binding appeal. The repetition of the schematic Chac mask becomes almost hypnotic in its effect; the viewer's focus blurs as it switches between unit and whole.

As at the Palace of the Governor at Uxmal, it is, obvious to the observer that techniques of mass production and division of labour have been applied here. The precision required for this extensive ornamentation could hardly have been obtained in any other way.

Perhaps the number of divine masks (260) was connected to the number of days in the sacred calendar of the Maya. In any case, the 45-metre long building is a stunning sight, with its five west-facing doorways leading into two rows of rooms and formerly surmounted by a *cresteria* decorated with openwork frets. It overlooks an artificial esplanade reached by a wide central staircase, leading to an altar, and rests on a base with a flight of steps running its entire width.

Inside the parallelipipedal building, the chamber occupying the centre of the façade displays an unusual feature. In order to enter the second chamber, a threshold of three steps must be crossed; these steps form a further mask of Chac arranged on the ground like a stepping stone. The nose in the form of a "trump" has been enlarged in order to simplify its transformation into ceremonial steps. It is displayed like a "rolled mat" – this the meaning of the Mayan name Codz Poop. In a certain sense, this motif laid out on the doorstep is related to the notion of rites of passage, in the same way as the doorways formed by gaping serpent's jaws found in buildings of the Chenes style.

To the east, the façade of another palace of Kabah faces east. This building has been the object of excavations and restoration which, in 1992, unearthed remarkable examples of large-scale statuary. These effigies, carved in the round, show full-length standing figures with a curious stylization of the human form giving an almost robotic quality. Stiff postures, schematic hands in the form of hooks, inexpressive features covered in ritual scarring and headdresses in the form of a crown make these carved limestone sculptures highly distinctive. It seems that they illustrate the worship of the Maya ruler at the end of the Classic period. A fragment of

A cluster of balusters
The Puuc-style palace of Chac-multún – on the border between the states of Campeche and Yucatán – bears the name of Cabal Pak and dates from the eighth to ninth centuries. Its decorative scheme is based on clusters of stone balusters bound by a central band.

one of these statues, on view in the Museum of Mexico, had indeed been dubbed the "King of Kabah".

Such statuary, set at a certain height against the façade of the palace, is somewhat reminiscent – *mutatus mutandis* – of the decoration of the pediments of temples in classical Antiquity. On a base that acts as a corbel or bracket, and surmounted by a mask of Chac which forms a sort of canopy, the work is flanked by similar effigies. The statues probably depict images of "deified" rulers; it seems unlikely that these images constitute a portrait gallery of mythical ancestors, though this cannot be ruled out. The sides of this building's door-frames are decorated with fine bas-relief scenes showing lordly plumed figures sporting elaborate hairstyles and carrying weapons and arrows. Here, too, the iconography seems to refer to specific historical events, rather than to mythology, as the decipherment of the hieroglyphic writing has revealed.

As in the majority of the Mayan sites already discussed, the palaces built at Kabah are set around raised esplanades. They enclose man-made terraces which are reached by sweeping flights of steps that lend cohesion to the layout of the city.

Puuc sobriety
The palace of Chacmultún, built on a strict plan, with cornices running around the whole façade and a line of balusters with two bands, was the residence of the Mayan priests of Yucatán. One should note, in the middle of the façade, the portico consisting of two monolithic columns topped with a square abacus.

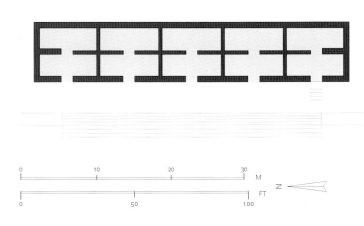

```
0        10        20        30   M
|----|----|----|----|----|----|
                              Z ←═
0           50          100   FT
|-----------|-----------|
```

Page 158
A royal threshold
Like a rug unrolled at the entrance
of a room of the Palace of Masks,
this step made in the image of the
god Chac demonstrates the
importance of the person who
lived in this palace.

Above
The Palace of Masks at Kabah
The Palace of Masks at Kabah, dating from the ninth century and
45 m long, was originally covered
in 260 identical effigies of the
god Chac. Set beneath a *cresteria*
formed of key patterns, the decorative scheme thus associated symbols of the sun with those of rain.

Below
Abundance and sobriety
The decoration of the Palace of
Masks at Kabah is exuberant,
but its basic conception is very
simple: the plan and elevation
of the building clearly show its
parallelepiped structure.

The statue of a ruler
Recently uncovered and restored to the façade of a palace of Kabah, this statue represents a Mayan king, actual size, above whose head rests a stone canopy in the form of a Chac mask. The work formed part of a "portrait gallery" of rulers.

Page 161
Chac omnipresent
Covering the façade of the Palace of Masks at Kabah, the effigies of the rain god present their repetitive faces in front of which their long crooked noses – like elephant trunks – form a curtain of stone.

Porticoed chamber
The palace of Sayil has many chambers that, in place of a door, present towards the exterior a wide portico with a pair of columns topped with a square abacus. The vaulting of the interior space possesses the shape of an arch with concave intrados.

The Great Palace of Sayil

Not far from Kabah, the site of Sayil is especially famous for its great three-storeyed stepped palace. The building stands on an area 85 by 40 m and includes, as at Edzná, an imposing central stairway. Its three flights lead to the seven doorways of the chambers on the highest level. The central opening leads into two chambers, one behind the other, whereas the six lateral chambers – three to the left and three to the right – each constitute a single vaulted space.

It is on the intermediate level – a sort of *piano nobile* – that the palace of Sayil contains the most interesting apartments. Instead of a simple square doorway, there is a wide aperture at the front of each dwelling in the form of a portico subdivided into three openings by a pair of columns. These round columns, either monolithic or in two sections, are surmounted by an abacus. They support a frieze peopled with gods – in particular with effigies of the "descending god" and of Chac, god of rain, as well as sky serpents represented in profile with gaping jaws. It should be pointed out that the descending god – who appears here and who crops up again at Tulum – is a strange representation of a mythical figure, depicted head down, with his body seen from behind and his legs in the air; the legs are bent like those of a toad. This

A monumental creation
Elevation and plan of the Palace of Sayil. The successive levels of the palace contained a large number of state rooms.

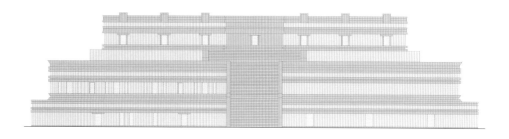

A three-storey palace
The Mayan site of Sayil, in Yucatán, is dominated by the bulk of the great palace, which is 85 m long. A central stairway links its three levels of vaulted rooms. Most of the columns in the porticoes of the second level are monolithic.

The haughty façade of Sayil
A view of the second and third
levels of the south-west wing of
the three-storey palace: on the
piano nobile, the pattern of
balusters with or without bands
and rooms with paired columns
features carvings that depict
the "descending god" flanked on
either side by monsters whose
jaws evoke those of the cayman.

The *Castillo* of Labna
At the top of a stepped pyramid
that seems to contain rooms
buried beneath the rubble of its
ruined façade, the sanctuary of
Labna, with its openwork *cresteria*,
dominates the Yucatec site. Of the
statuary that once ornamented it,
only the supports remain.

being, who seems to be plunging into the sea, is an image of the sun dropping toward the horizon. A such, it is situated on the side of the building touched by the last rays of the sun.

At window level, between the porticoes, rows of ringed balusters, closely juxtaposed in decorative sections, punctuate the façade, portraying in stone an architecture based on perishable materials. The cylinders of stone also contrive to highlight the friezes alternating their verticality with the horizontal forms of the deities. Lastly, small cylindrical elements, placed between two projecting bands, form cornices and mouldings that run round the whole façade. In addition to the highly stylized sculpted decoration, the proportions and outline of the building clearly derive from its wooden prototype, and that form the essence of the architectural ornamentation.

The Triumphal Arch of Labna

The Puuc city of Labna eventually spread over a huge area. Various buildings have been uncovered: a pyramid or *Castillo*, whose upper *cella* and high *cresteria* survive; several storeyed palaces which, like that of Sayil, include rooms with columned porticoes; and underground cisterns or *chultun*.

However, by far the most spectacular building on the site is doubtless a large monumental arch situated on a fortification at the foot of the *Castillo*. This symmetrical edifice, whose east-facing piers are decorated with a frieze of duplicated and reversed frets, has on its western side a series of small side rooms, and above these there are depictions of the traditional thatched hut in the middle of an open-work motif.

The arch itself consists of a single bay with a concave intrados – unlike the two great arches that link the wings to the central block in the Palace of the Governor at Uxmal, which are convex. The emblematic nature and solemn monumental appearance of this corbelled arch inevitably conjure up the image of a Roman triumphal arch. For we are not dealing here – as was the case in the Nunnery at Uxmal – with a simple passage leading into a *patio*, but rather with an imposing, even pompous, ceremonial construction which was solely intended to glorify either a site or person.

A balustered palace
The theme of "petrified" tree-trunks is present everywhere on the façade of the palace of Labna, whose vaulted rooms are arranged over several levels.

The main façade
While the back of the arch of
Labna is sober, the front is
covered with a symbolic decorative scheme. On either side of
the archway, doors open into
two small vaulted chambers.
Above them, the frieze shows huts
with a high thatched roof (the
standard Maya "house") beside
the criss-cross motif that imitates
the hut's lattice-work construction.

A true triumphal arch

Labna is renowned for its Mayan triumphal arch, whose appearance immediately recalls a Roman building: between the two lateral supports decorated by large key patterns, the vault with concave intrados forms a passage between two parts of the site.

A state monument

Elevation of the east and west façades and plan of the arch of Labna, which is in the Yucatán Puuc style.

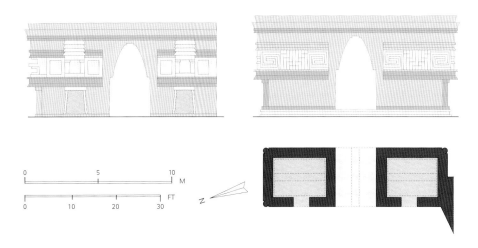

The Nunnery Pyramid
At the top of the Mayan building of Chichén Itzá that the conquering Spaniards named the Nunnery Pyramid, the block of the upper building unites a series of rooms beneath a mansard-style roof. The façades are decorated with lattice-work motifs and large key patterns.

Page 170
The *cenote* of Chichén Itzá
On the main site of the north-east of Yucatán, a collapse in the karstic surface has formed vast open-air water holes, known as *cenotes*. One of these natural pools, surrounded by scrub, was set aside for sacrifice: the priests hurled down offerings to the gods – in particular, young men and women sent to their deaths by drowning.

Chichén Itzá: pure Maya city

As the following chapter will make clear, there are two distinct periods of architectural activity in the city of Chichén Itzá which, under the influence of cultural currents imported by conquerors from the high Mexican plateaus, was to become the capital of Yucatán from the tenth century onwards.

The first of these phases is purely Mayan. Its works are in direct line of continuity with the Puuc style. Like the buildings of Uxmal, Kabah, Labna or Sayil, they feature friezes of balusters, masks of Chac, and open lattice-work ornamentation in stone. The second phase is marked by the intrusion of Toltec forms that radically transformed the architecture.

Situated in the centre of the north part of Yucatán, Chichén Itzá has two *cenotes*. One, which was inaccessible, was reserved for religious ceremonies, and in particular for the sacrifice of young people who were thrown down into it – dispatched directly to the gods of the Underworld. The other, named the cenote of Xtoloc, supplied the daily needs of the city's inhabitants. In fact, the presence of these "watering holes" in the karstic terrain was a blessing, providing water for the Maya who could thus provision themselves directly from the water table, which might otherwise have proved all but inaccessible.

The Nunnery and Iglesia

The names of certain Maya buildings come, like those at Uxmal, from the descriptions conferred on them by the first Spanish arrivals. The Nunnery and the Iglesia refer to two buildings of early Chichén Itzá, dating from the Maya period, which occupy the southern part of the site.

The Nunnery is a huge building that underwent several phases of construction. The main edifice is a high rectangular structure, comprising undecorated, quasi-vertical walls with rounded corners. A substantial stairway climbs the structure in a

Mayan Chichén Itzá
The buildings that stand by the Nunnery Pyramid – the annex, on the left and the small building known as the Iglesia, on the right – are characterized by a dense decorative style mixing elements of Chenes and Puuc styles.

single flight on the northern side. On the upper platform stands a palace displaying along its whole façade a design formed by four reversed fret motifs arranged on a background of balusters or cylinders. The side façades are covered in lattice-work mosaics. Instead of bearing a frieze, the roof inclines steeply, resembling the mansard-style roofs of Palenque. Another stairway leading to the top platform of this building, provides access to a third storey. The state of delapidation of this storey today prohibits public access.

To the east of the main building, forming an outbuilding of a very different style, is the most interesting element of the Nunnery. The forms here are a combination of the Puuc and Chenes styles. Again we find the central door beneath the gaping jaws and prominent fangs of the Cosmic Serpent. A frieze of Chac masks covers the walls and corners of the building. In the profusion of ornamentation encompassing the whole façade, from ground level to the top cornice, the central position in the frieze – as in the middle of the façade of the Palace of the Governor at Uxmal – is reserved for a sculpture very probably symbolizing the king, the deified sovereign. He is shown wearing a plumed headdress and sitting in majesty in the centre of a sort of "mandorla" or "glory" which expresses his religious influence.

Close by this building stands the Iglesia, a small single-chambered building resembling a rectangular chapel. With a very simple ground plan, its elevation displays a clarity the more remarkable amid the decorative exuberance of its neighbours: the lower level, which features a single doorway, is completely plain. Originally, even the stonework was probably hidden beneath a flat coat of stucco and whitewash.

At the level of the frieze, a band of frets extends below the large Chac masks over the door and at the corners. Above the projecting cornice stands the third section of the elevation, consisting of a high ornamental *cresteria*. It repeats in an open-work design the various motifs of the frieze – key patterns and Chac masks – as if to emphasize the ornamental scheme of the building.

A detailed examination of the finish of the decorative elements of the Iglesia reveals – as with the façade of the Nunnery outbuilding – that the frieze as well as the *crestaria* was once lavishly stuccoed and painted. It would seem that a thicker layer of plaster was applied at Chichén Itzá than at Uxmal and other Puuc sites. In all probability the architects of Chichén Itzá attempted in this way to conceal the black streaks characteristic of the local stone.

Prolific ornamentation
A detail of the Annexe and the Iglesia at Chichén Itzá. Everywhere there are masks of Chac and closely interwoven decorative motifs, on the cornices, friezes and sculpted panels.

The sovereign in the image of god
Above the doorway of the Nunnery Annexe at Chichén Itzá, the sovereign, wearing a plumed headdress, appears cross-legged, occupying the centre of a curious radiating motif that recalls the medieval mandorla. The "deification" of the Mayan prince is vigorously affirmed in this sculpture.

A wealth of symbols
Mayan art in its baroque manifestation: the cluttered façade of the Annexe of the Nunnery at Chichén Itzá borrows its large Chac masks from the Puuc style, whereas the set-back of the door, surmounted by fangs, evokes the jaws of the cosmic monster in the manner of the Chenes style.

**From the Iglesia
to the Observatory**
The back façade of the Iglesia of
Chichén Itzá displays profuse
ornamentation. It contrasts with
the bare terraces on which the
cylindrical tower of the Observatory stands.

The Caracol or Observatory of Chichén Itzá

Not far from the Nunnery, the visitor is surprised by the incongruous presence of a tall cylindrical structure – an unusual form in Maya architecture. Identified as an astronomical observatory, this building was christened *Caracol*, or snail, in view of its curious internal passageways.

The building stands on a platform 75 by 57 m which is itself surmounted by a terrace measuring 26 by 30 m. Two flights of stairs lead to the highly complex cylindrical structure. On a round base 18 m in diameter, the tower, covered in traditional Puuc-style friezes with projecting cornices, does not exceed 14 m in diameter and 11 m in height. The tower is itself surmounted by a lofty chamber where observations were made. This "watchtower" stands 28 m above ground level.

The construction of the *Caracol* tower deserves closer examination, as it contains a series of interesting technological and architectural innovations. The plan reveals three concentric cylinders separated by ring vaulting. The outer cylinder has four doorways placed at the cardinal points of the compass. A circular "corridor" sep- arates it from the middle cylinder which measures 8 m in diameter. This second circle has four doors in a quincunx arrangement in relation to those on the exterior. Like the first, it has a vaulted ceiling and contains a solid central core of masonry, in which a narrow spiral passage (which gives its name to the building) leads to the high chamber with spyholes in the walls.

Such is the building as interpreted by archaeologists in the first half of this century; one part of the observation chamber has since crumbled away. In fact, the three surviving "spyholes" provide enough information for it to be possible to

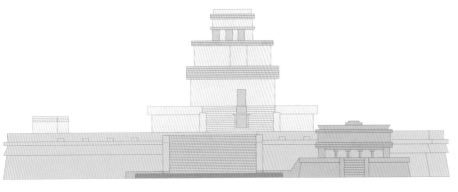

A circular plan

Elevation and plan of the astronomical Observatory of Chichén Itzá, or *Caracol* (snail): on terraces out of alignment with each other, the tower with its openings in a quincunx arrangement and the high chamber with observation spyholes form a complex radiocentric structure.

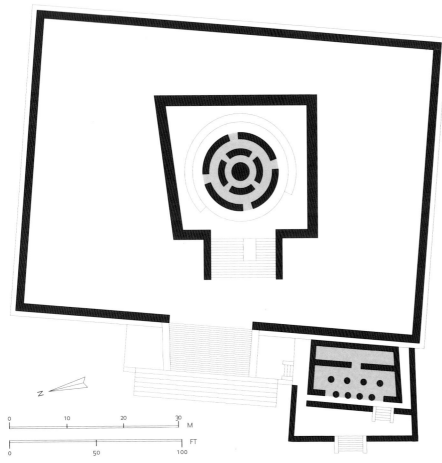

0 10 20 30 M

0 50 100 FT

**The creation of the
astronomer-priests**
From the summit of this tower, the
Mayan elite observed the stars in
order to establish an astronomical
calendar of great precision,
documented in codices such as the
Dresden codex (see page 15).

Concentric circles
Inside the tower of the Observatory at Chichén Itzá, the circular corbel-vaulted chambers observe a plan that includes staggered entrances. In the central cylinder, a spiral corridor – the *Caracol* that gave its name to the building – gives access to the high chamber.

understand the function of this observatory, which is justly celebrated as one of the major creations of Maya civilization.

The astronomical observations were made by examining the angle traced by light travelling along the "tunnel" formed by a long, narrow spyhole. Measurement of the angle between e.g. the right-hand edge of the external opening and the left-hand edge of the internal opening allow extremely precise observations to be made. By studying the evidence provided by the high chamber of the *Caracol*, we note that the first observation aperture faces directly towards the south, the second aligns with the setting of the Moon on 21 March; the third faces directly towards the West, and towards the point where the Sun sets at the equinoxes on 21 March and 21 September; lastly, a second viewpoint through the same "spyhole" corresponds to the setting of the Sun at the summer solstice on 21 June. These details are the foundations of the system: the X and Y upon which the more detailed observations of Maya astronomy are based. It is like a general orientation table, indispensable to further observations of the same kind.

Using this simple and, at the same time, very elaborate instrument – developed by an agrarian civilization barely out of the Neolithic period – the Maya obtained results of stunning precision (see below).

The lessons of the observation room

Section of the *Caracol* and plan of the high chamber with its three spyholes:

1. The south
2. The setting of the moon on the 21 March
3. The setting of the sun at the equinoxes
4. The setting of the sun at the summer solstice

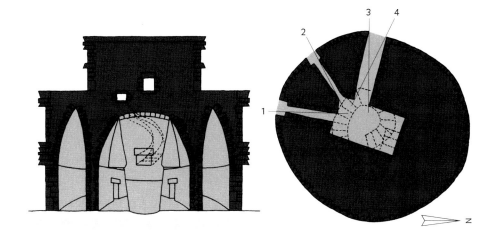

The tower of the *Caracol*

Over a door, the thick moulding that surrounds the cylindrical bulk of the Observatory of Chichén Itzá runs under a mask of the god Chac above which another moulding probably ran. At the top stands the observation room; one of the spyholes used by Mayan priests to examine the heavens can be seen.

Divinatory Astronomy

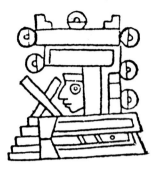 

Basic methods

The most complex instruments of observation used by the Maya were made of crossed rods, as is shown in illustrations in the codices. Nevertheless, the results they achieved were of extraordinary precision.

It was primarily to establish their highly complex calendar and to consult the disposition of the heavens for astrological purposes that the Maya observed the stars. In their desire to have increasingly accurate calculations and to read their future in the celestial constellations by predicting the appearance on the horizon of certain heavenly bodies, they developed an extraordinary science of astronomy.

Of course, this is a form of astronomy that limits itself to the visible movement of the stars, as was the case with all the great civilizations of Antiquity (Egyptian, Greek, Roman or Arab). It thus situates itself within a geocentric system – with the Earth occupying the centre of the universe.

The essential focus of their preoccupations was to fix the length of certain astral cycles with the utmost precision. With this in mind, the observations tended to identify simultaneity between two celestial events that repeated themselves when the same situation presented itself at regular intervals (e.g. the rise of the planet Venus, and the cycle of the Moon, as recorded in the solar calendar). It was mainly thanks to the Dresden Codex and the inscriptions at Copán that it became possible to reconstruct the discoveries of Maya astronomy.

As far as the solar year is concerned, the Maya were aware that the approximation provided by the 365 days of the calendar could be improved. Otherwise the system would be out of kilter. The Maya calculation based itself on 365.2420 days, whereas modern astronomers fix this same length of time to 365.2422 days. The error therefore is no more than 2/10000th of a day yearly, or 17.28 seconds. It had hardly any effect on the addition of a day every four years.

As regards the lunar cycle, we find two calculations: one covers 405 lunations, or 46 sacred "years" of 260 days, i.e. 11960 days. This period, by modern calculation, covers 11959.888 days. The Maya error is thus 0.112 of a day over a period of 32 years, which is the equivalent of 23 seconds per lunation. The other calculation is based on 4400 days per 149 lunations, which present-day astronomy calculates at 4400.0574 days, equivalent to 29.530587 days per lunation, whereas the Maya approximation corresponds to 29.53020 days. This calculation made in 682 by the astrologers of Copán contains a margin of error of 33.43 seconds per lunation.

To emphasize the visible nature of Maya astronomy, we should mention the Venusian year or cycle of Venus, which the Maya observers calculated to be 584 days, whereas modern calculation fixes the period at 583.92 days. But in its rotation around the Sun – a fact unknown to the Mesoamerican people – the planet Venus orbits in 224 days and 7 hours. The true cycle was therefore not taken into account.

In reality, it was the conjunction between 65 visible cycles of Venus and 104 solar years (a figure which represents twice the Maya "century" of 52 years) on the one hand, and 146 sacred years of 260 days on the other, that interested Maya astronomers.

How did the Maya, who possessed neither devices capable of measuring hours, minutes and seconds, nor observational instruments fitted with optical lenses and angular gradations, arrive at such results? The explanation lies in the fact that they relied on a very long series of observations – for example 384 years to establish the Venusian cycle – combined with arithmetical methods. In this way, major errors were eliminated, and reduced in proportion to the number of operations carried out.

As all this shows, the observational accuracy attained by the Maya exceeded their technological achievements. And the elements lacking in the Pre-Columbian culture had little if any repercussion for their calculations. On the contrary, one is struck by the way in which Maya society contrived to compensate for its technical deficiencies by simple methods – space, time, the number of workers, and the repetition of operations. This is the great lesson that emerges from an examination of the results achieved by the Maya in domains where they were indisputably ahead of the civilizations of the Old World.

Enthroned Mayan dignitary
Seated in majesty, this figure crowned with plumes and wearing fine attire is characteristic of Mayan nobility. Statuette in painted terracotta, 22 cm high, from the island of Jaïna. (Mexico City, National Museum of Anthropology)

Mayan warrior with shield
This statuette from Jaïna shows a figure wearing a large beaded necklace, a ruff and a long coat. He holds a rectangular shield in his left hand and probably once held a spear in the right. The funerary statuettes of Jaïna date from the late Classic and the Postclassic periods. (Mexico City, National Museum of Anthropology)

THE CONTRIBUTION OF MEXICO TO YUCATÁN

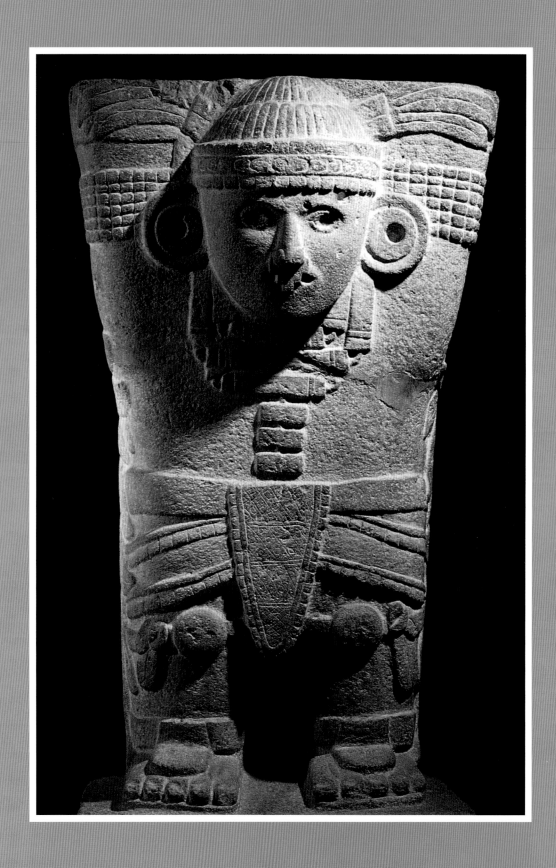

Chichén Itzá – Capital of the Toltec-Maya

Page 183

Disk of turquoise mosaic
Discovered on the back of the red Jaguar, in the first Castillo of Chichén Itzá, and dating from the eleventh century, this disk of serpent motifs in turquoise and coral is a Toltec-Mayan work. In the centre was probably a pyrite mirror used during a solar fire ritual. (Mexico City, National Museum of Anthropology)

Atlantean figure of the Temple of Warriors
A series of sculptures of this type supported the sacrificial altar that stands at the top of the Temple of Warriors at Chichén Itzá. 88 cm tall, this Toltec-Mayan work probably dates from the end of the eleventh or the twelfth century. (Mexico City, National Museum of Anthropology)

In discussing the city of Tikal in Guatemala, we described the penetration into the Petén region of an architectural influence originating from the great city of Teotihuacan on the high Mexican plateaus. One manifestation of this was that the *talud-tablero* characteristic of the central regions began to appear in certain Maya buildings. This was a consequence of the migration of peoples originally from Teotihuacan who had reached the Petén lowlands. These events seem to be contemporary with the war waged around A.D. 375 by Tikal against Uaxactún.

Following the great upheavals caused by waves of invading semi-nomadic tribes from the semi-arid zones of northern Mexico, the settled peoples of the great cities of Mesoamerica were destabilised. In Europe, a similar and contemporary phenomenon occurred: the great invasions that caused the fall of the Roman empire. In Mexico, whole "nations", hounded by invaders, took flight and gradually sought safety further south, particularly in the lands occupied by the Maya. The influences that they brought with them were not simply artistic. Since art and religion were so closely linked among the pre-Columbian peoples, this could hardly be. Their cultural influence was felt in the emergence in Maya society of Tlaloc, the god of rain from Teotihuacan.

A similar wave of migrations took place at the end of the tenth century, with the arrival – whether it was gradual or sudden we simply do not know – of groups of warriors hailing from the city of Tula. This was the capital of the Toltecs, the masters of the upland regions of Mexico. These groups began to encroach into Maya territory. The new arrivals settled at Chichén Itzá and made it their new capital. On this site, occupied by the Maya who had built Puuc-style edifices there, they built a magnificent new city.

Should we see a link between the influx of Mexican peoples into Maya land and the invasion of the Chichimecs – plundering nomads of Mexican origin, who pillaged Tula for the first time in the tenth century? It is not impossible. This interpretation receives some degree of support from Toltec sources which allude to calamitous events. Before 987 – perhaps earlier according to certain sources – it would seem that a proportion of the inhabitants of Tula abandoned the capital. These Toltecs, under the leadership of their chief Topilzin – who would henceforth go under the name of Quetzalcoatl, like the Plumed Serpent known in Yucatán as Kukulkán – are thought to have wandered aimlessly. They are known to have passed through Vera Cruz and Tabasco. After reaching the Maya lands of Chiapas, where the Classic cities had already been abandoned, they settled in the north of the Yucatán peninsula, and made Chichén Itzá their home.

Whether it be legend, myth or romanticized historical tradition, the struggle that took place between Topilzin and his brother Tezcatlipoca (who bears the title of Warlord of the Toltecs – and later of the Aztecs) would seem to mirror the upheavals that drove certain groups of the population into exile. As a result, they "colonized" Chichén Itzá, a city which from that time forth experienced an extraordinary renaissance.

Toltec Influence

This new Chichén Itzá was the result of a merger between the architectural traditions of the Maya and those of the Toltecs of Tula. It was long thought that the Toltecs were responsible for the introduction into Maya land of the bloody rituals and human sacrifice characteristic of the Mexicas. This was not the case; as we have seen, the tribes of the Petén, Chiapas and Yucatán already practised blood offerings and the execution of sacrificial victims. Nevertheless, the militaristic character of the Nahua-speaking peoples (the language of the Aztecs) certainly accentuated these violent tendencies.

The Toltecs, whose socio-political system was wholly governed by the warrior orders of Eagles, Jaguars and Coyotes, imbued their art with a dramatic, bloody character. On the bas-reliefs decorating the Toltec-Mayan monuments of Chichén Itzá, motifs featuring the skulls of ritual victims, eagles and jaguars devouring hearts, and armed warriors bearing the decapitated heads of the vanquished abound. Aesthetic concerns changed. Death was present everywhere.

But the Toltec religion was not the only element to pervade Maya territory. Architecture, sculpture and decoration underwent a deep change as the cultures interpenetrated. And the main monuments of the Toltec-Mayan Chichén Itzá bear the imprint of the forms, the spatial relationships, and functions that originated in Tula. Construction techniques were modified to meet new ritual and spatial requirements. This particularly applied to the sanctuaries intended for the solemn assemblies of members of military orders. The men belonging to the "brotherhoods" of Eagles and Jaguars needed vast covered areas in which to hold their assemblies. Religion was no longer the exclusive territory of high priests and rulers: it became the prerogative of the warrior-caste that now held power.

Other types of buildings continued to develop, such as the pyramid and the ball court traditional not only to Maya culture but to many other pre-Columbian peoples of Mesoamerica. The Toltec imprint is less evident in these constructions. Above all, the technique of the corbelled roof, a Mayan speciality, was maintained. The traditional concrete vault was sometimes combined with new forms: this occurred, for

The centre of Chichén Itzá
The Toltec-Mayan buildings that flourished under the influence of traditions from the northern Mexican plateaus made Chichén Itzá one of the most splendid Pre-Columbian capitals: on the left, the Temple of Warriors; on the right, the Pyramid of the *Castillo*.

example, in the Court of the Thousand Columns and in the Temple of the Warriors. Highly original hypostyle spaces resulted from this development.

It is therefore a mixed, hybrid architecture that arose during the Toltec-Mayan renaissance of Yucatán. Hybrid, however, is by no means synonymous with stylistically weak, indeterminate or shapeless. Indeed, the reverse was true: benefiting from the contributions of both peoples, the art that flourished in the late Chichén Itzá demonstrates enormous progress in spatial and aesthetic terms, and also expressed a profound formal transformation. It transcends the forms of both the traditions from which it issued.

A huge metropolis

The ceremonial centre of Chichén Itzá includes a wealth of impressive monuments:

1. Cenote of sacrifice
2. Ball court
3. Tzompantli
4. Platform of Venus
5. Castillo
6. Temple of the Warriors
7. Columned structure/Group of the Thousand Columns
8. Market square
9. Pyramid of the High Priest
10. Cenote of Xtoloc
11. Caracol
12. Nunnery Pyramid

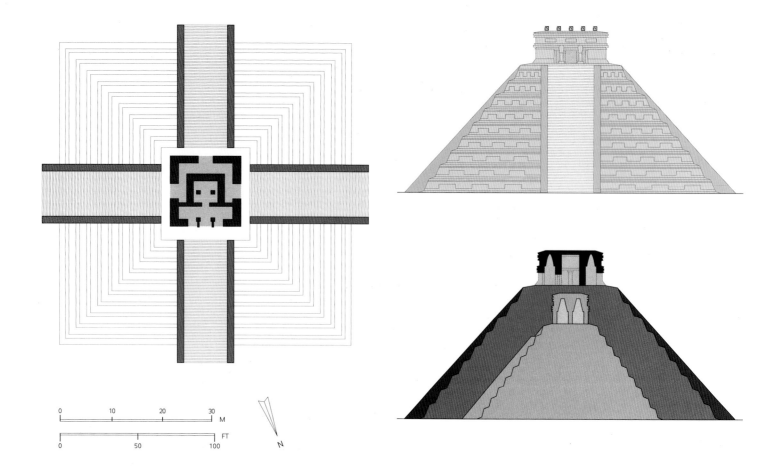

Toltec-Maya Monuments

At the centre of the city of Chichén Itzá is the *Castillo*: the Great Pyramid of Kukulkan. It has a symmetrical ground plan measuring 55 m on each side, covering 3000 m² and reaching a height of 30 m. Four large stairways climb the pyramid, flanked by string walls at the base of which we see, on the north side, two sets of Plumed Serpent's jaws.

Each stairway has 91 steps, making 364 in total; the threshold at the entrance of the upper sanctuary represents the 365th day of the solar year. The nine stepped levels bear a meandering relief which probably imitates the coils of the Cosmic Serpent.

The upper sanctuary, set back southwards in order to accommodate a ritual area in front of the entrance, has a triple bay whose two columns depict the body of a snake, with its jaws forming the base at ground level, the body forming the shaft and the tail with its rattlesnake scales raised against the upper frieze, according to a tradition from Tula that symbolizes Quetzalcoatl. The vaulted oblong vestibule leads to a "holy of holies". Inside, two pillars support the roof with lintels made of sapodilla wood. This marks an important innovation in roofing techniques. Other buildings of Chichén Itzá also featured this development. On the three sides that surround the *cella*, a surrounding vaulted gallery isolated the inner sanctum within the high temple.

The investigations undertaken by archaeologists within the body of the pyramid during restoration works on the *Castillo* proved highly successful: in the centre of the outer construction, they discovered a more ancient pyramid (once again, the principle of superposition). This was a square structure measuring 30 m on each side with a platform 16 m high. Under the masonry of the building covering it, the older

A square pyramid

The *Castillo* of Chichén Itzá, with its sanctuary to which four central stairways climb. Plan, elevation and section showing the first *Castillo* (tenth and eleventh centuries) that has survived beneath the building visible today, the result of a superposition.

The Great Pyramid of Chichén Itzá
Between the square pillars of the Temple of Warriors, we see the symmetrical outline of the *Castillo*. The right hand part of the pyramid has been fully restored; the left has been cleared of vegetation but is otherwise untouched.

pyramid was intact: its upper sanctuary, accessible by a stairway climbing the north side, formed two vaulted chambers, one behind the other – following the long-established Maya tradition.

When this discovery was made, this sanctuary still contained the remains of the last rituals that had been held there. At the entrance, the visitor encounters a votive altar in the form of a statue. It represents a figure lying on its back, with legs folded up and torso raised, leaning on the elbows. On its belly was a hollowed, shallow basin intended to receive the offerings of the Toltec rituals: namely, hearts ripped from the chests of sacrificial victims, or the decapitated heads of ball players. This style of statue, originally from Tula, is known by the name of Chac Mool, after the sovereign who was thought by those who first discovered it to be represented. This picturesque name now defines a genre.

In the centre of the second chamber of the sanctuary at the top of this first *Castillo*, archaeologists made a surprising find: a stone throne carved in the form of a jaguar painted red and incrusted with green jade segments representing the markings of the beast's coat. The animal – part-sculpture, part-furnishing – has its head turned towards the door – just as the Chac Mool does. It terrifies anyone entering with its menacing fanged jaws and protruding spherical green eyes. It was probably intended to awe those who attended the ceremonies over which the ruler of Chichén Itzá presided, sitting on this throne.

Whereas the first Toltec-Mayan pyramid of Chichén Itzá dates back to the very late tenth century or the beginning of the eleventh, the second *Castillo* cannot be later than the second half of the eleventh century or the early twelfth century, since the city seems to have been abandoned at a date close to A.D. 1200.

The model of the *Castillo* or Temple of Kukulkan was reproduced on a smaller

The throne of the Red Jaguar
Discovered by the archaeologists when the sanctuary of the first *Castillo* was opened, this throne in the form of a wild beast is decorated with jade motifs, ivory fangs and pyrite eyes.

The sanctuary of the *Castillo*
At the top of the pyramid of Chichén Itzá, the *cella* illustrates the progress of architecture in the Toltec-Mayan period: instead of a tiny internal space, the hall is composed of three naves with a vaulted roof supported by square pillars.

The jaws of the plumed serpent
The gaping jaws that prohibit access to the steps of the *Castillo* belong to a deity of Toltec origin.

The Pyramid of the High Priest
In the manner of the *Castillo*, this recently restored building at Chichén Itzá includes four central stairways preceded by the menacing jaws of the plumed serpent.

scale in Toltec-Mayan Chichén Itzá to create the so-called Temple of the High Priest, which has recently been extensively restored. This smaller version has four central stairways in the form of plumed serpents, whose open jaws frame the base of the sloping string walls.

Likewise built on the principle of double axial symmetry, two small structures decorate the ceremonial centre: the platform of the Eagles and Jaguars and the platform dedicated to the planet Venus. Both constructions are reached by four stairways guarded by jaguar-heads at the top of the string walls. The façades are decorated with sculpted panels depicting the mythological Eagles and Jaguars devouring hearts, and symbols of the planet Venus.

Another larger platform (50 m long) is built on a plan in the shape of a short-tailed "T". Probably an annexe to the nearby ball court it was designed for a macabre purpose: when the teams came off the ball court, the heads of the decapitated victims were deposited there. Known as *Tzompantli*, this Platform of the Skulls is entirely decorated with skulls which lend it a funereal and sinister character, singularly appropriate to the death-dealing nature of the Toltec religion.

A protective image

As if to protect the entrance of the sacred buildings, a menacing beast stands at the top of the stairs of the platform dedicated to the planet Venus, whose visible planetary cycle was of great importance in the Mayan calender.

In honour of the planet Venus

The Morning Star and the Evening Star – two aspects of the planet Venus – gave rise, at specific dates, to rituals and sacrifices that seem to have been carried out at the summit of this platform, reached by a flight of fourteen steps.

The *Tzompantli* or the Platform of the Skulls
The sanguinary nature of the Toltec-Mayan religion is expressed by this building on which the priests came to deposit tens – even hundreds of severed human heads. Thus exposed, the heads of the vanquished – prisoners of war or losers at the ball game – were sacrificed to the gods to sate their thirst for blood.

The fascination with death
The frieze of *Tzompantli* expresses without equivocation its function. Standing close to the ball court of Chichén Itzá, it displays a sort of morbid exultation at the image of death.

The Temple of the Warriors

The huge complex known as the Temple of the Warriors is the most important grouping at Chichén Itzá. It is also the one which most clearly shows the influence of the Toltecs on Yucatán, for its general arrangement derives directly from the main temple of Tula. This was the sanctuary of Tlahuizcalpantecuhtli dedicated to the Planet Venus as Morning Star. This incarnation of Venus (Venus is also the Evening Star) was incarnated by Quetzalcoatl.

How was the Toltec-Mayan sanctuary of Chichén Itzá arranged? It consisted of a pyramid supporting a large square *cella*, which was reached by a central stairway that ended at the upper terrace opposite a large stone Chac Mool. The statue was positioned in front of the entrance portico which took the form of two large rattlesnakes, their gaping jaws flush with the ground and their erect tails bearing the lintel.

This pyramid was composed of four stepped levels in *talud-tablero* form; its sides are covered in reliefs that depict the symbols of the orders of Eagles and Jaguars alongside ritual scenes.

At the foot of the building, a quadruple pillared portico led into a vast hypostyle hall composed of three bays. Of the structure of this hall, there remain today only sixty square roof-supports; the vaults have collapsed. This covered space was extended laterally by the covered Court of the Thousand Columns.

Here at Chichén Itzá we have a replica, faithful to the last detail, of the model provided by the temple at Tula. The very same elements are present: the main body of the pyramid supporting a vast upper sanctuary; the positioning of a Chac Mool at the entrance; the Eagles and Jaguars in heraldic "passant" pose that decorated the

The Temple of Warriors of Chichén Itzá
Preceded by a triple colonnade whose stonework vaults have collapsed, the sanctuary, looks over the great square of the Toltec Mayan metropolis. A Chac Mool stands guard at the summit of the access stairs.

An impressive complex
In the unchanging scrubland of
Yucatán, the Temple of Warriors,
flanked by the Thousand Columns,
displays the refinement and the
monumentality of the twelfth-
century Toltec-Mayan architecture
found at Chichén Itzá. On the
left, under the hillock, lies a small
un-excavated pyramid.

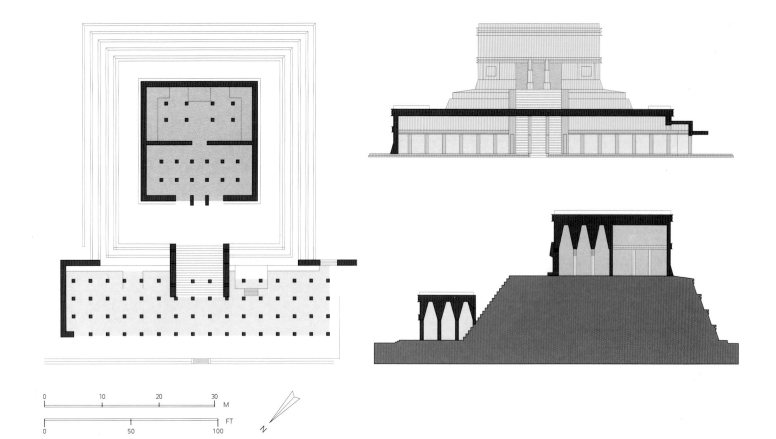

Chichén Itzá: the Temple of Warriors
Plan, elevation of the façade and section of the Toltec-Mayan edifice. The size of the upper sanctuary relative to the pyramid is much greater than that of the *cella* at Tikal.

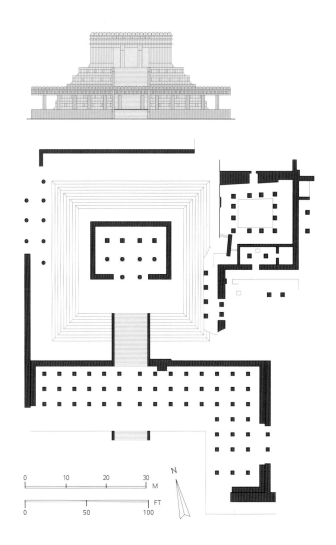

Tula: the Temple of Tlahuizcalpantecuhtli
On the northern Mexican plateau, the Toltec city of Tula and its Temple of the Morning Star provided the model for Chichén Itzá, the "Super-Tula" in Yucatán. A comparison of the two plans is very revealing.

A Toltec warrior

Coming down from the mountainous centre of Mexico, the Toltec army took over the Mayan land in the north of Yucatán, establishing its sanguinary practices there.

Levels covered in reliefs

The structure of the Temple of the Warriors, reverting to the principle of the *talud-tablero* (bank and panel created in Teotihuacán), facilitated the creation of great friezes exalting the power of the military orders of the Eagles and the Jaguars.

Jaguars devouring hearts

On the reliefs of Chichén Itzá, jaguars feed on human hearts ripped from the chests of their victims. At their side, masked warriors adopt the posture of Chac Mool.

projecting elements of the *talud-tablero*; the same snake-shaped pillars depicting rattlesnakes, with head and jaws flush with the ground, bodies forming the shaft and erect rattle supporting the lintel of the entrance portico. Finally, at the foot of the pyramidal mass, there is the same hypostyle hall with several bays and multiple supports.

When the Toltecs reached Chichén Itzá, they decided to build a sort of "Super-Tula" to recreate their original sanctuary. It is worth pointing out, however, that the Temple of the Warriors at Chichén Itzá had been preceded, as with the *Castillo*, by an earlier building now buried in the body of the main construction: an earlier temple at the top of a similar, but much smaller, structure has been discovered. It presents characteristics that the later superposed building repeated. This earlier version already employed the Maya technique of concrete vaulting over the pillared porticoes of stone. It seems evident that the newcomers immediately adopted Maya methods of construction. The difference between the two temples is one significant detail: instead of the single transversal row of pillars in each of the two chambers (hallway and inner sanctum) present in the earlier version, the later version featured a double portico running crosswise. This shows that the builders had the courage to create larger inner areas resting on light, slender supports.

Assembly areas of considerable size were created during this final phase of the architecture of Yucatán. The ritual needs of the warriors led to the creation of huge hypostyle halls. The bays of the hall stretching in front of the Temple of the Warriors covered an area 50 m by 12 m: 600 m² in all – whereas the main hall of the Palace of the Governor in Uxmal did not exceed 80 m². The hall continued with a wing 110 m long, set at right angles, thus covering more than 1400 m², while the other hypostyle wing, flanking the south side of the pyramid, has almost the same total area. This group, known as the Court of the Thousand Columns, has no less than 200 square pillars and round columns, which once supported concrete vaults supported by wooden lintels.

For the audacity of the architects of Chichén Itzá lay in the combination of the numerous pillars and columns of the Toltec tradition with the great stone vaults of Maya architecture. In this configuration, the corbelled concrete ceilings no longer rested on walls but on free-standing shafts. By using transversal beams to link the numerous stone supports, it was possible to create hypostyle halls of unprecedented size.

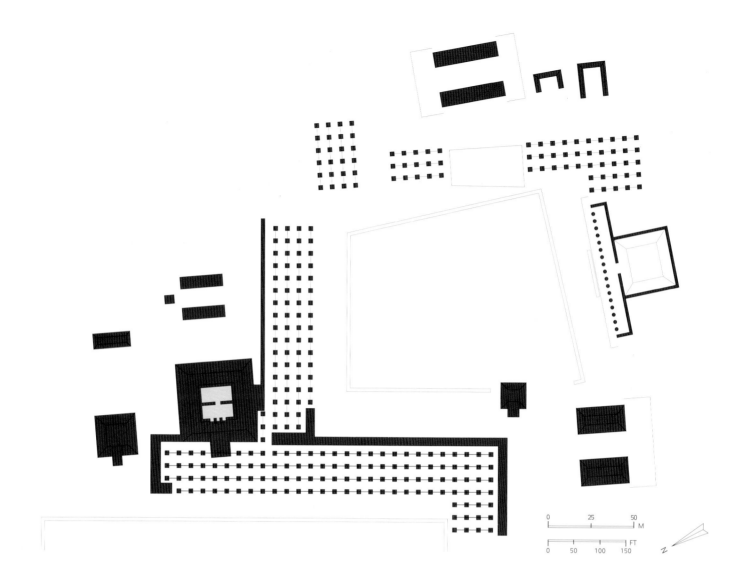

The complex of the Thousand Columns
Plan of the area surrounding the Temple of Warriors at Chichén Itzá: several colonnades, comprising three or four bays, are arranged around a trapezoid square, flanked by a ball court and by a porticoed building thought to be the Market.

The colonnade by the pyramid
Cylindrical columns, constructed of several superposed stone drums, originally supported the stonework vaulted ceiling. The bays collapsed when the wooden architraves rotted.

Column shafts as far as the eye can see

The view over the Thousand Columns unfolds in front of the *Castillo* of Chichén Itzá: Toltec-Mayan architecture had now mastered the vast internal spaces needed for the assemblies of warriors.

The *atrium* of the Market

Supported by high cylindrical columns, the *atrium* of the Market of Chichén Itzá once surrounded an elegant *patio*. This light structure, topped by a roof frame in the form of a *compluvium*, created a fine urban space.

It was an elegant formula. But if the lintels of sapodilla wood burnt or rotted, the whole ceiling caved in, taking with it pillars and columns. In this respect, the price of Toltec-Maya innovation and technological progress was greatly increased fragility. The consequence was that none of the great vaulted hypostyle halls of Chichén Itzá have survived intact.

Extending southwards from the Thousand Columns, there is a symmetrical structure 75 m wide forming a vestibule lined by a portico. This entrance stands in front of a covered square area, surrounded by a colonnade which creates a sort of *impluvium*. Supported by extremely elegant lofty columns, a roof made of palms laid over a wooden frame surrounded this open-air *patio*. Known as the *Mercado* or Market, this airy edifice repeats and refines the centripetal formula of the *patios* of Tula used for assemblies of warriors.

As we can see from these examples, a veritable host of roofed areas existed in Chichén Itzá at the time of the Postclassic Toltec-Maya. At the end of the Maya civilization, architecture reached the height of its achievement by endowing Yucatec art with a series of interior spaces the like of which no pre-Columbian people had ever known. They were probably surpassed only by the palatial constructions of the Aztecs, about which unfortunately little is known, since their discovery by the armies of Cortés was immediately followed in 1522 by their total destruction when Tenochtitlán was razed by the Spanish conquistadors.

On this subject, we should note that one type of building had completely disappeared in Toltec-Maya Chichén Itzá: the palace, or stone dwelling. No new edifices with living quarters were built, no rows of apartments were arranged in quadrangles. Had the new masters of Yucatán adopted, as the sole abode of their elite, the old Nunnery complex? Or were the war chiefs and the "nobles", returning to ancestral traditions, content to live in huts made of mud and palms?

On the other hand, in matters of hygiene – probably associated with purification rites – the new Chichén Itzá had small vaulted steam baths that demonstrate the concern for cleanliness of the Amerindian peoples living in the tropics.

Areas for tribal meetings
These columned structures – the hypostyle halls of the Toltec-Maya – reveal a deep change in the customs of the people, with the emergence of new needs imported from central Mexico.

The Great Ball Court

The finest ball court ever built by the pre-Columbians is certainly that of Toltec-Maya Chichén Itzá. The complex covers around 160 by 75 m on a north/south axis. The pitch itself covers 7 000 m². Its traditional ground plan in the form of a flattened letter "H" is flanked by banks and 8 metre-high walls whose wide flat surface served as a seating area for spectators. The complex also includes a series of buildings: to the east, there stands a sanctuary known as the Temple of the Jaguars facing outwards; above it, the Temple of the Tigers, which faces inwards, overlooks the arena where the teams did battle; lastly, at each end, stands with vaulted roofs probably accommodated the political and religious "dignitaries" of the city.

The low banks on either side of the ball court bear instructive sculpted bas-relief carvings in which the ceremony held after the game is depicted. The iconographic interest of these records lies in their depiction of the team captains in their ceremonial dress or match attire; the later decapitation of the beaten victim with jets of blood shown spurting from the slit neck, and the head of the executed man still wearing his headdress and decorations. The whole scene focuses on a huge skull depicted in profile against a disk, one positioned at the centre of each of the two banks adjoining to the ball court. Above it, perpendicular to the surface of the lateral walls, a ring of stone juts out 7 m from ground level on each side: it was through the openings of these "goals" that the gum ball had to pass. Each ring is decorated with a carving representing two entwined snakes fighting.

The Temple of the Tigers, overlooking the ball court at the southern end of the eastern bank, has a two-room sanctuary. At the back, the vault of the dark inner sanctum was covered with lively battle scenes. In front, three bays lead into the vestibule. This portico is subdivided by two Plumed Serpents. At ground level their jaws gape open. Their cylindrical bodies and tails (the horny scales of the rattle are clearly visible) are held aloft to form genuine columns rather than square pillars. These sculptures foreshadow, in a somewhat clumsy style, the theme to which the entrance of the Temple of the Warriors, probably of later date, gave perfect sculptural expression.

At the foot of this structure, on its eastern side, on the threshold of the Temple of the Jaguars, there stands a stone throne in the form of a stylized jaguar, to which

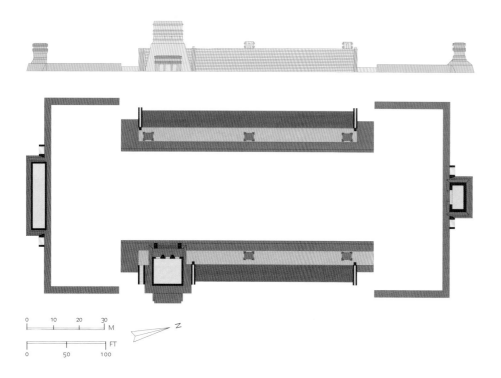

the temple owes its name. The temple's inner walls are decorated with fine carved reliefs showing mythological scenes of the ritual practised in this consecrated enclosure.

The association of sanctuaries with the ball court leaves no doubt as to the religious character of this Maya "sport": the pitch itself is nothing less than a representation of the universe, the sacred place where the eternal struggle between light and darkness takes place, where the stars, Sun and Moon orbit under the watchful eye of the master of Xibalba, the Lord of the Underworld.

Above

The meandering of the snake
The ring of stone that constitutes the "goal", on each side of the sports field at Chichén Itzá, is dedicated to the Plumed Serpent, the famous Kukulkan imported into Yucatán by the Toltecs, who called it Quetzalcoatl.

Page 206 below

Here, fights to the death took place

Longitudinal elevation and plan of the large ball court of Chichén Itzá, 160 m long. On this area 7 000 m², the players pursued the sacred game of the Toltec-Maya, with padded belt, gum ball and body armour. The defeated team was sacrificed to the gods.

Page 206–207

The ball court and the Temple of the Tigers

Seen from the top of the *Castillo* of Chichén Itzá, the court constitutes a vast structure of which only part can be seen here. The monument is on the same scale as the immense landscape of the Yucatec jungle that stretches as far as the eye can see. The Temple of the Jaguars, overlooked by the Temple of the Tigers, places the Mayan sport under the aegis of the gods.

Adjoining a pyramid

The portico of the Temple of the Jaguars displays the general characteristics of Puuc style. Inside, the shallow relief carvings (hardly distinguishable) illustrate the phases of the Toltec migration.

The jaguar still awaits his priest

In front of the vaulted area, the stone jaguar forms a throne that recalls – in more primitive style – the one discovered in the first *Castillo*.

A pavilion for the dignitaries?
At the northern end of the ball court, a stand probably received the elite of the military-religious Toltec-Maya society of Chichén Itzá.

Beneath the symbol of death
A shallow relief placed in the centre of the ball court, on the sloping wall of the banks on either side, represents a death head that leaves no doubt as to the destiny of the vanquished team during cosmological contests.

The proud façade of the sanctuary
A temple of deadly kind. Dedicated to the emblematic Tigers of the tribes, it overlooked the sanguinary rituals of the Toltec-Maya ball court of Chichén Itzá.

Page 211
The venerated plumed serpents
The entrance of the Temple of the Tigers is decorated – like that of the Temple of Warriors – with paired columns in the form of rattlesnakes. With their jaws open at ground level and their tails raised, they support the superstructure of the building.

The drawing of Catherwood

The interest of the general public for Amerindian art began with the "reportage" of the American traveller John L. Stephens and the talented artist Frederick Catherwood. Between 1838 and 1842, they travelled through Mayan lands, describing the sites, and extended their research as far as Honduras. At Chichén Itzá, Catherwood's views – executed with the help of a *camera lucida*, a forerunner of the camera – accurately recorded the riches of the site.

Above: This view of the Annexe of the Nunnery, with the Iglesia on the right, demonstrates the reliability of Catherwood's vision. *Below:* The *Castillo* before it was cleared of vegetation and underwent an exemplary restoration.

Catherwood's engravings illustrated Stephen's accounts, and were reprinted in many editions. They possess undeniable charm.

Above left: the interior view of the sanctuary of the *Castillo* of Chichén Itzá is proof of the accuracy of the drawing (compare the photograph on page 190).
Below left: the *Caracol* or Observatory of Chichén Itzá, still overgrown with trees.

Above right: in the maritime city of Tulum, the *Castillo* with perfectly preserved steps.
Below right: a building at Tulum surrounded by the forest of Quintana Roo.

CONCLUSION

Decline and Fall of the Maya Civilization

Last incarnation of Chac
This painted terracotta, 21 cm high, from Mayapan, dates from the Postclassic period. It shows the rain god in human guise, but for the fangs visible at the corners of his mouth. (Merida, Museum of Merida)

Polychrome incense-burner
Composed of several assembled, painted pieces, this terracotta from Mayapan represents the rain god under the guise of a richly attired bearer of offerings and dates from the last Mayan period. (Mexico City, National Museum of Anthropolgy)

One of the mysteries which has fascinated historians of the pre-Columbian world is the reason why the Maya civilization disappeared. Its decline mystifies the authors who have studied this very advanced culture. Specialists have come up with the most varied of reasons to explain it, and we shall consider some of them at the conclusion of this study.

For now, it may be helpful to outline the phases of this decadence. It was punctuated by final bursts of energy, as if the peoples who had pursued such a glorious destiny and left such fabulous traces of their achievements, had sought to postpone the fatal hour.

The Charm of Tulum

Tulum is among the most attractive of the late Maya cities – in part due to its surroundings. This fortified settlement, built in the north-east of Yucatán, stands intact in the middle of an enchanting landscape on the shore of the Caribbean sea. Its temples survey cliffs that plunge into turquoise waters hemmed by beaches of white sand produced by a coral reef.

This city is so late that one of the Spanish conquistadors, Juan de Grijalva, skirting the shores of Yucatán in 1518, reported that he had seen this city from afar. But, not daring to cross the breakers at the reef which prevented his ship from landing, he was unable to approach it. Dazzled by the charm of a vision akin to a mirage, he did not hesitate to compare Tulum with Seville. If we stick to the evidence, however, Grijalva had embroidered reality, for the monuments of Tulum, though highly original, are minor ones. The most remarkable feature is really the outstanding site: the sea-front temples of Tulum take on the appearance of a tropical Cape Sounion. But their bulky silhouettes, rough-hewn masonry and rudimentary volumes do not confirm this first impression.

In effect, this is late Postclassic architecture; it dates from between the thirteenth and the late fifteenth centuries and clearly shows the influence of Chichén Itzá and its columned halls. But the *Castillo*, or main temple, with its great stairways flanked by sloping string walls and its sanctuary preceded by three bays carried on stonework columns inspired by the pillars of the Toltec-Maya, is a building without elegance or finesse. Its coarse stone finish must have been covered by a rendering of polychrome plaster.

The most interesting structure is the Temple of the Frescoes, with its five-bayed entrance portico divided by four thick columns. Behind this doorway, which is surmounted by effigies of the descending god, a vaulted hall has preserved the paintings covering its vaulted ceiling. In greys and blues, they imitate the style of contemporary manuscripts – in particular certain Mixtec codices from Oaxaca – and once again demonstrate the influence of the culture of the Mexican uplands on the peninsula of Yucatán.

On the outside, stylized masks of Chac mark the corners of the friezes. Here stucco is integral to the design. This last incarnation of the god of rain, with its pro-

truding fangs, no longer possesses the long nose of the god K. The style of the temple is akin to that of a building from a much earlier epoch, that is the Temple of the Seven Dolls at Dzibilchaltún.

Facing this cumbersome and hasty construction, we are struck by the strong incline of the walls. They slope outwards: the superposed friezes project one above the other and seem to defy the law of gravity.

The parallel alignments governing Tulum's urban plan and habitat have been firmly established by archaeologists. The city is surrounded by a dry stone wall that measures 450 m from north to south, and approximately 150 m from east to west. On its seaward east-facing side, the vertical cliffs incessantly pounded by the breakers offered adequate defences. A creek allowed trading canoes to land easily on the shore of Quintana Roo, and from there several routes led across the scrub to Chichén Itzá and Cobá.

At the other end of the Maya world, the city of Iximché, founded in the fifteenth century by the Cakchiquel tribe from highland Guatemala, offers a further example of the final era. The considerable vestiges of this fortified city, built in 1470, are situated 2 260 m above sea-level. By 1524, it had been destroyed by the conquistador Pedro de Alvarado. But here, as at Tulum, we perceive the last dying embers of the Maya civilization. Six centuries earlier, the Classic metropolises had begun to

The *Castillo* of Tulum
The "apse" of the main building at Tulum, dating from the Post-classic period, when hybrid architecture had replaced the purer early styles.

The Great Pyramid of Tulum

While the overall impression of the *Castillo*, built on the edge of the cliffs of Tulum, is still striking, the construction work is no longer of quality; the finish is irregular and the stonework careless. At the top, the sanctuary contains a *cella* in front of which stand cylindrical columns.

General plan of Tulum

On the edge of the Caribbean sea and surrounded by walls that complement the natural defences of the high cliffs, the site of Tulum is composed of a series of secondary sanctuaries arranged around the central *Castillo*.

1. Main entrance
2. Temple of the Frescoes
3. *Castillo*

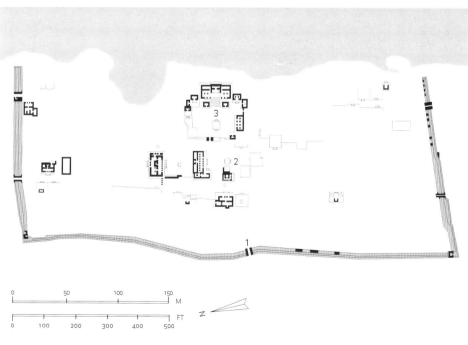

More beautiful than Seville
Sailing along the coast of Yucatán in 1518 – before Cortés landed in Mexico – Juan de Grijalva was deeply impressed by the city of Tulum. Here the descendants of a great but declining civilization had settled. Grijalva did not make the mistake of landing. He knew that the Maya were a bellicose nation.

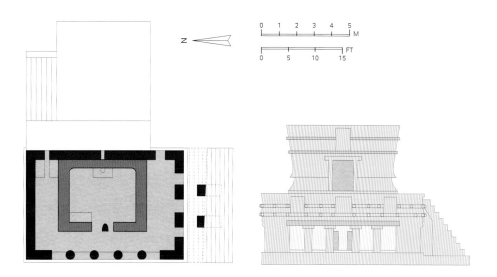

The Temple of the Frescoes

Above left: Plan and elevation of the façade of the Temple of the Frescoes at Tulum.

Above right: detail of the stucco reliefs of Chac decorating the corners of the sanctuary.

Below: with its haphazard architecture and awkward forms, Tulum bears the stamp of decline. The Temple of the Frescoes, with its clumsy stonework columns and undulating frieze, is the expression of a moribund world.

Like a look-out on the sea front
This small sanctuary annexe dominates the cliffs of Tulum. Its outward sloping walls are characteristic of the final period of the Mayan builders.

The frescoes of Tulum
The traces of Postclassic paintings that survive inside the Temple of Frescoes of Tulum represent stylized deities – following the model of late Mexican manuscripts. We are now a long way from the Classic pictorial forms of Bonampak.

The *Castillo* of Coba
Not yet cleared of the invading
vegetation, the *Castillo* of Coba
dominates a region of lakes.
A perfectly straight sacred Mayan
road, or *Sacbé*, joined Coba to
the city of Yaxuna, around 100 km
away.

disappear. Blame for this attaches equally to the encroaching tropical forest of the
Petén and Chiapas and the barbarian invaders; the cities that were pillaged were,
however, already on the decline. Little by little, these once prestigious centres were
forgotten, invaded by the luxuriant vegetation that submerged their masterpieces
in a sea of green.

For when Grijalva spotted the inhabitants of the coasts of Yucatán, almost five
hundred years – half a millennium – had passed since Tikal, Copán and Palenque had
foundered beneath the rainforest that had rapidly reclaimed the lands once cultivated by the Maya.

The Decline of the Maya Cities

The death-throes of the Classic metropolises built in the Petén, Chiapas, Belize
and Honduras are reflected in the sudden cessation of inscriptions: the dating of
monuments gradually comes to a halt at each of the Mayan sites, without any clear
reason.

We should note that stelae and lintels become rarer and disappear from 790
onwards. The last date at Bonampak is 795. At Palenque it is 799; at Yaxchilán, it is
808; at Quiriguá and Piedras Negras, 810; at Copán, 820; at Machaquila, 841; at

Altar de Sacrificios, 849; at Tikal, 879; at Seibal, 889; and at Chichén Itzá, 898. It is at Tonina that we find the last date calculated in the Long Count: 909.

So in little more than a century, the brilliant cultural organization of the Maya disappeared. Their traditions sank into oblivion and, one by one, the tribes entered a period of decline.

What happened? To answer this question, archaeologists and historians have posited various hypotheses, invoking epidemics, mass uprisings, flooding and the inexorable invasion of the forest. They have suggested climatic changes, the abandonment of lands and lack of maintenance of the drainage canals, which would have resulted in massive plagues of malaria. They also mention revolutions pure and simple, which could have been caused by the over-exploitation of the work force. They also blame the constant inter-tribal wars which weakened the central power of the "provinces", the huge number of human sacrifices, which might have led to depopulation and consequently to famine if the agricultural workforce was weakened.

All these causes did perhaps bring about the decline of the Maya. It is possible, indeed, that they combined to cause the final cataclysm. But the main reason would seem to lie, once again, in population movements that originated in the semidesert wastes of northern Mexico. Barbarian tribes displaced the civilized "nations" who took flight to escape annihilation.

Entire peoples migrated, and we know that their tribes – Pipils, Putuns, Quichés and Toltecs – invaded Maya territory. When the old native society, which had become disorganized and weakened, was faced with uncivilized warmongering nomads, it collapsed despite its indisputable superiority; for nothing came to re-place its institutions. On the other hand, when the settled populations fled before invading hordes, the arrival in Maya territory of highly cultivated bands of warriors

A late Mayan city: Iximché
During the great migrations of populations that coincided with the end of the Mayan era, the tribe of the Cakchiqueles built a short-lived capital called Iximché on the highlands of Guatemala (at an altitude of 2260 m): built in 1470, it was destroyed in 1524 by the Spanish. Nevertheless, it contains powerful structures built on a sacred area organized around an orthogonal plan.

**A funerary urn of the
Quiché-Maya**
Among the best ceramicists of the
Mayan world, the newly arrived
tribe of the Quichés, who settled
on the highlands at the end of the
Classic period, created large
painted funerary urns. This detail
of a work from Nebaj reveals a
remarkable sense of form.
(Guatemala City, Popol Vuh
Museum)

produced a final golden age, as the apogee of Toltec-Maya Chichén Itzá demonstrates.

In addition to the displacements caused by the great invasions from the north, other factors must be taken into consideration. These almost certainly include external influences caused by the patterns of trade established during the ninth and tenth centuries along the new trade routes that covered central America. Thus the impact of gold-working – whose arrival was contemporary with the birth of the Toltec-Maya period – threw the foundations of Maya society into question. Such events imply far-reaching socio-political upheavals and strike at the very cultural and religious underpinning of a society. They heralded fundamental changes and the ensuing disruption may have undermined civic, spiritual and moral values, calling into question the cohesion of the Maya world. The causes of their decline were indeed manifold. Faced with the death of a whole civilization, it seems scarcely possible to favour one hypothesis over another.

We should bear in mind that the last descendants of the Maya encountered by the Spanish at the beginning of the sixteenth century had little in common with the astronomers and the architects who founded the great urban centres in the virgin forest. They were no longer part of the élite intelligentsia who had been responsible, five centuries earlier, for the golden age of the pre-Columbian world. Small, hurriedly constructed cities alone offered a semblance of past splendours. By contrast, the great Classic buildings survived, like vast skeletons submerged in the jungle, amid the ruins of what had once been an astounding urban civilisation. Oblivion threw its veil over the abandoned and delapidated Maya capitals. And slowly, the roots of mighty forest trees burst the walls, vaults and palaces once lived in by the representatives of a brilliant élite of scholars and artists.

The Architectural Legacy

Over eight centuries, from the dawn of the modern era until the end of the late
Classic period in the middle of the ninth century, Maya architecture achieved considerable advances. Progressing from massive, flat platforms to tall pyramidal constructions that towered high over the forest, it never ceased to develop, using
the resources of stonework and of concrete. Similarly, from the early inner areas of
the stone-roofed sanctuaries with their tiny vaulted chambers, to the ceremonial
halls of the great palaces, Mayan architecture constantly enriched its formal vocab-
ulary and building techniques. The large scale of construction that it achieved,
represented the advancement of knowledge, the growth of power and the affirmation of an emblematic art peculiar to the people who created it.

In the metropolises of the virgin forest, the soaring pyramids and the long
narrow palace dwellings formed the spatial elements of a complex sculptural urban
language that employed esplanades, squares, quadrangles, symmetrical and asymmetrical perspectives and processional thoroughfares along rectilinear ceremonial
avenues.

This architecture, whose works proliferated in dozens of cities, displayed not
only a wide diversity of forms but also the continuity of particular elements: every
city possessed pyramidal sanctuaries, multi-chambered palaces and ball courts.
Buildings were placed on artificial substructures, studded with stelae and altars.
These complexes – often defined as ceremonial centres – were organized according
to the rules imposed by a sophisticated liturgy.

Observatories, platforms for worship and sacrifice, fortifications, tombs and
crypts were in due course added to this initial list of buildings. But this repertory
names only the solid, stone-built backbone of Maya architecture. The dwelling
of the common people was the traditional mud hut with its palm roof. Only the elite
received stone accommodation.

In addition, Mayan architectural art included a vast repertory of bas relief, sculpture and painting. The creations decorating the buildings make Maya architecture
one of the essential "documents" of a civilization which little documentary evi-

dence has survived. This is why the monuments play an essential role in our understanding of the mentality of a people whose state of knowledge continues to surprise us.

In the tenth century, at the very end of the Maya period, the invasion of the Toltec tribes from Mexico enriched the architecture with new themes, and in particular with vast meeting halls for members of warrior orders. Resulting from a combination, on the one hand, of flat roofs supported by stone pillars or columns, such as existed at Tula, and on the other hand, of the corbelled concrete vault characteristic of the Classic Maya, this architectural revolution, represented by the solid roofed hypostyle hall with long parallel bays whose vaults buttress each other, made a considerable impact.

With its supreme mastery of internal spaces, Toltec-Maya architecture represents the apotheosis of pre-Columbian America. And paradoxically, it was born at a time when, elsewhere, Maya civilization had already been dealt a mortal blow.

A vigorous expressionism
Quiché-Mayan pottery achieved a style of remarkable power in funerary urns that reproduced the effigies of deities modelled in the round. (Guatemala City, Popol Vuh Museum)

CHRONOLOGICAL TABLE

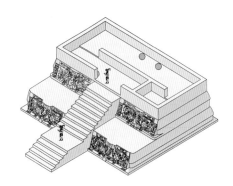

Reconstruction of the
first temple at Cerros (Belize)

Monuments

1000–400 B.C.
    La Venta
300 B.C.–A.D. 150
    Kaminaljuyú
A.D. 156   La Mojarra, Stela
A.D. 36   El Baul, Stela
A.D. 50   Cerros, Structure 5C-2
c. A.D. 1–50 Uaxactún, E-VII Sub

300	Uaxactún, H-Sub 3
Sixth century	Tikal, Temple IV
Seventh century	
	Pyramid of Great Jaguar
734	Tikal, Tomb of Great Jaguar
762	Copán, Stands
545–757	Copán, Stairs
810	Copán, last stela

672–720	Palenque, Palace
675	Palenque, Temple of the Inscriptions
690	Palenque, Temple of the Sun
692	Palenque, Temple of the Cross
720	Yaxchilán, Shield-Jaguar Lintel
792	Bonampak, frescoes

2000 B.C.–A.D. 300	A.D. 300–900	A.D. 300–900
Archaic to Preclassic	**Classic – Petén/Belize**	**Classic – Chiapas**

2000–1200 B.C.
    Archaic
1200–900 B.C.
    Early Preclassic
900–300 B.C.
    Middle Preclassic
300 B.C.–A.D. 300
    Late Preclassic

375	Teotihuacán influence on Tikal
378	Uaxactún-Tikal war
534-593	Chronological hiatus

320	Beginning of Yaxchilán dynasty
431	Beginning of Palenque dynasty
605	Birth of Pacal
640	Death of Queen Zak Kuk
683	Death of Pacal
684–702	Reign of Chan Balum
795	Final date at Bonampak
799	Final date at Palenque
808	Final date at Yaxchilán

Historical Events

The great pyramid of Tikal,
named Temple I

The funerary crypt of the Temple
of the Inscriptions at Palenque

Stucco mask from the main pyramid at Kohunlich

Façade of the Temple of the warriors at Chichén Itzá

Fourth–fifth centuries		Fourth century			
	Kohunlich, Temple of the Masks		Dzibilchaltún, Temple of Seven Dolls	Late tenth – early eleventh century	Chichén Itzá, First *Castillo*
550–700	Chicanna, Structure I	569	Uxmal, Pyramid of the Magician	Late eleventh century	
c. 600	Becan, Fortifications	649	Uxmal, Ball Court		Chichén Itzá, Second *Castillo*
800–850	Becan, Temples	879	Chichén Itzá, Lintel	c. 1200	Mayapan founded
672–810	Edzná, Stelae				

A.D. 300–900
Classic – Campeche/Quintana Roo

A.D. 300–900
Classic – Yucatán

A.D. 900–1524
Postclassic – Yucatán

830	End of activity at Chicanna

909	Chichén Itzá, Caracol, final Mayan date

950–1000	Toltec invasion; Chichén-Itzá occupied
c. 1200	Quiché tribe settle
c. 1200–1250	Chichén Itzá abandoned
Thirteenth century	
	Migrations of the Cakchikel
1470	Iximché founded
1518	Grijalva sees Tulum
1524	Destruction of Iximché

Chenes-style façade in the form of a mask, Structure II at Chicanna

The great staircase of the pyramid of the Magician at Uxmal

The pyramid of the *Castillo* at Tulum

Glossary

Abacus: Horizontal, flat architectural element placed at the top of a pillar or column.

Altar: In Mayan society, sacrificial altars were sometimes associated with stelae. Carved out of a monolith, they often took the form of monsters and earth deities.

Amerindian: Inhabitant of Pre-Columbian America. A term employed to make the word "Indian" more precise; it was conferred on the inhabitants of the New World by Christopher Columbus – who thought that he had landed in India when he reached the Caribbean islands.

Baktun: Mayan chronological terminology for a period of 144 000 days, equivalent to 394.5 years.

Ball game: Team sport widely played in Pre-Columbian cultures from the Olmec to the Aztec period. Its territory covers Mesoamerica, from El Salvador to the semi-arid regions of Northern Mexico. It was a "sacred" sport that was played with a large ball of solid latex. It required considerable skill as the opponents were allowed to use neither their arms nor legs to touch the ball. Only the torso and hips could be used. The game was played on vast walled and banked playing areas. Goals in the form of stone rings or stelas were placed around the court . At the end of the "match", a player could be sacrificed to the gods – either by decapitation or cardiectomy.

Caracol: From the Spanish for "snail", it designates a circular construction at Chichén Itzá consisting of a spiral staircase. This building was an observatory, constructed in order to make astronomical readings.

Castillo: From the Spanish "small castle", the term is often applied to the principal building of a Mayan city (pyramid of Chichén Itzá, temple of Tulum).

Ceiba: The biggest tree of the rain forest. By extension, the sacred tree which formed the axis of the universe in Mayan cosmology.

Cella: Term borrowed from Latin to designate the inner sanctum of a temple, where sacrifices and the main religious rituals were enacted.

Cenote: From the Mayan term "Dzonot", an open-air natural well, formed by the collapse of the limestone layer, which gives access to the underground water table.

Ceremonial centre: Term often used by archaeologists to denote the ensemble of stone buildings of a Mayan city, where rituals and sacrifices took place.

Ceremonial rod: Insignia of power held by Mayan dignitaries. It consisted of a large sceptre, often decorated at each end with the heads of monsters.

Chac Mool: Term created by the nineteenth century French explorer Le Plongeon to designate a style of Toltec-Mayan statue that has a round disc on its belly for the purpose of receiving offerings. The Chac Mool is a recumbent figure with its legs drawn up and its torso supported on its elbows.

Chenes: Region of the Yucatán peninsula that is situated between the Puuc region of the North and the Río Bec region near to the Guatemalan frontier. The term refers to an architectural style characterised by lavish ornamentation. Structure I on the site of Chicanna is a particularly characteristic example.

Chultún: Mayan term for a reservoir excavated in the hollow of a valley for the purpose of seasonal irrigation.

Codex: Mayan manuscripts made from the bark of the amate tree. The pages open up like a folding screen. Some of these books reach a length of 13 m.

Coffering: The casing into which cement is poured. Mayan builders made coffering out of stone. The blocks, equipped with tenons protruding inwards from the wall, were fixed in the concrete mass. This permanent coffering formed the visible outer casing.

Concrete/cement: Building material used by the Maya in their vaulting construction: the liquid mortar mixed with rubble was poured into a permanent casing that performed the role of coffering. The concrete formed a monolithic mass.

Corbel vault: Among the peoples of central America (from the North of Mexico to Costa Rica), the Maya were the only one to use the arch and the vault. These were, however, corbel vaults or arches, built up horizontally, unlike true vaulting, which makes use of voussoirs.

Coyotes (Order of): Warriors of the Toltecs, Toltec-Maya and later the Aztecs grouped under the symbol of the Coyote, or American jackal. See also Eagles and Jaguars.

Cresteria: Spanish name given to the roof-comb on Mayan buildings. It consisted of an ornamental construction – often formed from two open-work walls leaning against each other – on which relief sculptures were placed (stucco figures or key patterns). This lofty decorative addition was intended to lighten the appearance of a sanctuary or palace.

Eagles (Order of): In Toltec and Toltec-Mayan society (and later in Aztec society), the Eagles were a group of warriors connected by their special status: they were military-religious dignitaries.

Glyphs: Term, analogous to Egyptian hieroglyphs, referring to the complex symbols of Mayan writing. The glyph is composed of one or two primary elements to which prefixes or suffixes are often appended.

Intrados: Inner curve of an arch, or interior concave surface of a vault.

Itzas: Name of the tribe from the northern plateaux who, after passing through the region of the Gulf, invaded Yucatán, together with the Putuns, in the tenth century.

Jade: Semi-precious stone, usually green, with which several other minerals of the same colour are associated, such as nepheline and jadeite. The colour green, symbol of life for the Olmecs and the Maya, was considered to possess magical powers. Jewellery and masks made of jade were placed in the tomb of a dead sovereign. They were thought to protect the dead man.

Jaguars (Order of): Grouping of warriors in Toltec, Toltec-Mayan and Aztec society; it formed the elite of the Mexica race. Members of the Order of the Jaguars, like those of the Order of the Eagles, played an active role in the campaigns waged to provide a supply of sacrificial victims.

Katun: Period of 7 200 days in the Mayan calendar, or slightly less than 20 years.

Kin: A day in the Mayan calendar. The unit of the chronological system.

Lintel: Horizontal supporting element in stone or in wood closing off the upper part of a door or bay. The Maya often made lintels out of sapodilla wood. In certain cities of the classic period (Yaxchilán), stone lintels were richly carved on their front or lower face.

Long Count: System of Mayan date calculation based on five figures called *baktuns, katuns, tuns, uinals* and *kins,* starting from an initial date corresponding to 3113 B.C.

Mansard roof: The roofs of certain Mayan buildings (Palenque, Yaxchilán) are described by this feature of French classical architecture which comprises a double incline, of which the lower is steeply inclined, and the upper almost flat. The lower incline was sometimes decorated with painted stucco reliefs.

Mask: Decorative element used to cover the face of buried dignitaries. The gods also wore masks whose emblematic nature facilitated the combination of several deities.

Mesoamerica: An area situated approximately between the present-day United States border and Costa Rica.

Mexica: This term designates the Pre-Columbian tribes that spoke the Nahuatl tongue, such as the Aztecs and their predecessors, the Toltecs.

Morning Star and Evening Star: See under Venus.

Nahuas (Nahuatl): Ethnic group from Mexico speaking the Nahuatl tongue, including the Toltecs and the Aztecs, equally known as Mexicas.

Neolithic (revolution): Progressive evolution of the techniques of animal husbandry, agriculture and pottery that occurred when the previously nomadic, hunter-gatherer prehistoric tribes began to settle (from 5000 B.C. onwards).

Obsidian: Natural magmatic glass used instead of flint for the manufacture of tools and arms by peoples without metallurgical technology. Knives, arrow-heads and spears were made out of this material. With their great skill in carving, the Maya made true works of art in obsidian, such as large complex sceptres, carved out of a single piece of this volcanic stone.

Olmecs: Modern term, meaning "men of the land of rubber", that refers to the population of the first advanced civilization of Mesoamerica, emerging around 1500 B.C. in the region of the Mexican Gulf (Tabasco and Vera Cruz today). The Olmec civilization, "mother of the arts", established the characteristics of the Amerindian world of Mexico: the pyramid, ball court, hieroglyphic writing and statuary were all invented by them.

Orthostats: Slabs standing at the base of a wall.

Patio: Spanish term for a small interior court.

Portico: Gallery on pillars or columns.

Pre-Columbian (Pre-Conquest): Designates the civilizations that existed in America before the arrival in 1492 of Christopher Columbus in the New World. Pre-Conquest designates the peoples of Mesoamerica before the conquest of Mexico by Cortés in 1522.

Puuc: Zone where Mayan architecture flourished in the northwest of Yucatán at the end of the Classic period (650–900). The term comes from the name of the hills in this Mayan region.

Pyramid: Architectural structure in the form of a cone or truncated cone. In Pre-Columbian society, a sanctuary stood at the top of the pyramids. In the Mayan world, pyramids often contained a subterranean tomb (crypt of the Pyramid of the Inscriptions at Palenque).

Quetzal: Bird of the tropical forest whose intensely green feathers were highly prized for the ritual and emblematic attire of the Mayan dignitaries.

Rattlesnake: A snake representing the deity Quetzalcoatl, or the Plumed Serpent, who originated among the Pre-Columbian civilizations from the northern plateaux (the inhabitants of Teotihuacan and then the Toltecs of Tula). These peoples introduced the cult into Mayan territory in the Post-Classic period.

Río Bec: The region to the south west of Yucatán on the border of Guatemala and Belize that gave rise to an original architectural style, whose heavy and complex ornamentation formed illusionistic structures. The buildings imitated the towers of the pyramids: their steeply inclined stairways could not be climbed and the high sanctuary was purely symbolic, with a solid mass masquerading as the door to the *cella*.

Sacbé (pl. sacbéob): Meaning "white road" in Mayan, a term referring to the rectilinear, skilfully-levelled processional routes that linked certain Mayan cities, sometimes over dozens of kilometres.

Sapodilla: A tree whose wood was valued by the Maya for its durability and resistance to rot.

They used it to build the lintels of palaces and temples.

Sierra: Mountain in Spanish. The zone of the *sierras* in Mayan territory is mainly situated along the Pacific coast of Guatemala where large volcanoes are still active.

Stela: Large standing stone, usually decorated with carved reliefs and glyphic inscriptions. Mayan stelae served to commemorate historical or religious events. The sculpted decoration generally depicted a ruler performing a ritual.

Stucco: Plaster with natural resin (and sometimes fibre) added that was used by the Maya for the sculpted decoration of their stone buildings: pillars, roofs, *cresterias* were covered in reliefs made of painted stucco.

Talud-tablero: Architectural formula with a sloping lower wall surmounted by a rectangular panel with projecting framework. This device made up the levels of pyramids in the architecture of the great city of Teotihuacan in the northern plateaux of Mexico, and its influence is seen in the monuments of Tikal in the fourth century A.D.

T'ao T'ie (or taotie): Refers to a type of Chinese mask depicting monsters or fantastic animals, constructed on a rigidly symmetrical format with emphasis given to the eyes, ears and jaws. Decoration of Chinese archaic bronzes which are similar to the Chac masks of the Puuc style.

Tumulus: Artificial earth and stone mound usually containing a tomb.

Tun: Period of 360 days in the Mayan calendar.

Tzompantli: Aztec term for the altar where the heads of decapitated sacrificial victims were deposited.

Uinal: Period of 20 days in the Mayan calendar. 18 *uinals* make up a *tun* of 360 days.

Venus: Planet of the solar system to which the Maya and other Pre-Columbian peoples of Mesoamerica attached great importance in the ritual of death and resurrection. In its incarnations as Evening Star and Morning Star, it represents the transition from the mortal world to the after-life.

Vigesimal system: In Mayan mathematics, the system of notation is positional: its base is the number 20. Consequently, one changes column after 19, 399, 7 999, that is to say at the twentieth unit, the tenth, the hundredth etc.

Wisconsin (glaciation): The American appellation corresponding to the Wurm glaciation in the West. This fourth and last glaciation period occured between 80 000 and 10 000 B.C.

Xibalba: Kingdom of the Underworld or Afterlife of the Maya, according to the text of *Popol Vuh.*

Zapotecs: Pre-Columbian people from the region of Oaxaca (capital: Monte Alban). Their flourished civilization was between A.D. 250 and 800.

Zero: Mathematical sign denoting a numerical value of nought. In Mayan mathematics, the positional notation gave rise to a specific sign in the form of a shell symbolising zero.

BIBLIOGRAPHY

Adams, Richard E.W., Walter E. **Brown** and T. Patrick **Culbert:** "Radar Mapping, Archaeology, and Ancient Maya Land Use", *Science,* 213, 1981.

Alcina, José: *L'Art précolombien,* Paris 1978.

Andrews, E. and V. **Wyllis** in: "Dzibilchaltún", *Supplement to the Handbook of Middle American Indians,* 1, Austin, Texas, 1981.

Art Millénaire des Amériques, with contributions from Jean-Paul Barbier, Iris Barry, Conceisao G. Corrêa etc., Geneva, 1992

Art précolombien du Mexique, catalogue of exibition in the Galéries Nationales du Grand Palais, Paris, 1990.

Berlin, Heinrich: *Signos y significados en las inscripciones mayas,* Instituto nacional del Patrimonio cultural de Guatemala, Guatemala City, 1977

Baudez, Claude-François and Pierre **Becquelin:** *Les Mayas,* Paris, 1984.

Baudez, Claude and Sydney **Picasso:** *Les Cités perdues des Mayas,* Paris 1987.

Carrasco Vargas, Ramon: *Chicanna, Campeche, Un Sitio de la Frontera Sur – Estudio arquitectónico,* UNAM, Mexico, 1994.

Coe, Michael D.: *Breaking the Maya Code,* London, 1992.

Coe, Michael D.: *Les Mayas – Mille ans de splendeur d'un peuple,* Paris, 1987.

Culbert, T. Patrick (ed.): *Classic Maya political history, Hieroglyphic and Archaeological Evidence,* with contributions from Norman Hammond, Peter Mathews, Linda Schele etc., A School of American Research Book, Cambridge, New York, 1991.

Grube, Nicolai: *A preliminary Report on the Monuments and Inscriptions of La Milpa, Orange Walk, Belize,* Baessler-Archiv, Berlin, 1994–1995.

Hartung, Horst: *Die Zeremonialzentren der Maya,* Graz, 1971.

Hellmuth, Nicholas M.: *Pre-Columbian Ballgame, Archaeology and Architecture,* Guatemala City, 1975.

Kowalski, Jeff Karl: *The House of the Governor – a Maya Palace at Uxmal, Yucatán, Mexico,* Norman, 1987.

Leyenaar, Ted J.J. and Lee A. **Parson:** *ULAMA – The Ballgame of the Mayas and Aztecs,* Leiden, 1988.

Marquina, Ignacio, *Arquitectura prehispanica* INAH, Mexico, 1951.

Miller, Virginia E.: *The Frieze of the Palace of the Stuccoes, Acanceh, Yucatán,* Dumbarton Oaks Research Library and Collection, Washington D.C., 1991.

Morley, Sylvanus G.: *La Civilisación Maya,* Mexico, 1961.

Proskouriakoff, Tatiana: Olmec and Maya Art – Problems of their stylistic relations, in: *Dumbarton Oaks Conference on the Olmec,* Washington D.C., 1968.

Robertson, Merle Greene: *The Sculpture of Palenque,* 4 vols., Princeton, New Jersey, 1983–1991.

Ruz Lhuillier, Alberto: *Costumbres funerarias de los antiguos Mayas,* Mexico, 1968, reprinted 1991.

Schele, Linda and Mary Ellen **Miller:** *The Blood of Kings – Dynasty and Ritual in Maya Art,* Kimbell Art Museum, Fort Worth, 1986.

Schele, Linda and David **Friedel:** *A Forest of Kings, The Untold Story of the Ancient Maya,* New York, 1990.

Soustelle, Jacques: *Les Mayas,* Paris, 1982.

Stierlin, Henri: L'Art Maya – des Olmèques aux Mayas-Toltèques, Fribourg, Paris, 1981.

Stierlin, Henri: *Maya,* Architecture universelle, Fribourg, 1964.

Stierlin, Henri: *L'Or et la Cendre – A la rencontre des Amériques, 1492,* Paris 1991.

Stierlin, Henri: "Les surprises de l'art précolombien", *L'Oeil,* 454, 1993.

Stuart, David and Stephen **Houston:** *Classic Maya Place Names,* Dumbarton Oaks Research Library and Collection, Washington D.C., 1994.

Taube, Karl Andreas: *The major Gods of Ancient Yucatán,* Dumbarton Oaks Research Library and Collection, Washington D.C., 1992.

Thompson, J. Eric: *Grandeur et décadence de la civilisation maya,* Paris, 1958.

Die Welt der Maya, catalogue of exhibition at Cologne, Eve and Arne Eggebrecht, Nicolai Grube, Karin v. Welck (Ed.), Mainz, 1994.

INDEX – Monuments

INDEX – Persons

ACKNOWLEDGEMENTS AND CREDITS

The author and the publisher are most grateful to the Mexican authorities — and in particular to the Tourist Bureau, SECTUR — for their help with the photographic assignments undertaken for this book. The photographers are especially grateful to the Director, Mr. Juan Manuel Buendia, to the Deputy Director, Mrs. Victoria Orozco Ito, and to Mr. Bernard Forat, who organized their travels with such painstaking care.

Mention must also be made of the kindness extended by the Aeromexico Company, and by Mr. Fiorenzo Zanni, its Director in Paris, for the facilities provided on the Paris-Cancun-Mexico lines.

Lastly, Anne and Henri Stierlin took all the photographs in Mexico, Guatemala and Honduras, except for a handful of documents, for which they are grateful to the following archives:

Pages 27, 48, 50, 51, 52 left: © Arturo Braun, Mexico.

Pages 46, 47, 49, 52 right, 53, 54 above left and right: © Maximilien Bruggmann, Yverdon.

Pages 44/45: © André Martin, Paris.

Page 10: NASA, Washington.

Pages 130, 133, 174 below: © Matteo Vercelloni, Milan.

We should like to offer our special thanks to Mr. Alberto Berengo Gardin for producing the plans on pages 11, 24, 28, 38, 42, 43, 46, 48, 53, 55, 71, 75, 78, 83, 88, 90, 106, 112, 118, 128, 129, 133, 137, 146, 159, 163, 169, 176, 179, 187, 188, 198, 202, 206, 219, 222.

THERE'S GOING
TO BE A BABY

*With love to
Klara and Emil*

H. O.

First published 2010 by Walker Books Ltd
87 Vauxhall Walk, London SE11 5HJ

2 4 6 8 10 9 7 5 3 1

Text © 2010 John Burningham
Illustrations © 2010 Helen Oxenbury

The right of John Burningham and Helen Oxenbury
to be identified as author and illustrator respectively of this work
has been asserted by them in accordance with the
Copyright, Designs and Patents Act 1988

This book has been typeset in Polymer
Printed in China

British Library Cataloguing in Publication Data:
a catalogue record for this book is available from the British Library

ISBN 978-0-7445-4996-6

www.walker.co.uk

WALKER BOOKS
AND SUBSIDIARIES
LONDON • BOSTON • SYDNEY • AUCKLAND

There's Going to Be a Baby

John Burningham
Helen Oxenbury

There's going to be a baby.

When is the baby going to come?

The baby will arrive when it's ready, in the autumn, when the leaves are turning brown and falling.

What will we call the baby?

If it's a little girl I'd like to call it Susan or Josephine or perhaps Jennifer.

I hope it's a boy, so we can play together, boys' games, and I think it should be called Peter or Spiderman.

What will the baby do?

Maybe the baby
will work in the
kitchen and
perhaps be
a chef.

I don't think
I'd eat anything
that was made
by the baby.

Maybe the baby will grow up to be an artist and paint lovely pictures.

If the baby is an artist, don't let it paint pictures in our house. It will make a terrible mess everywhere.

Perhaps the baby will
be a gardener and
make things grow.

When the
baby's bigger,
it can play
with me.

Mummy, can't you
tell the baby to go away?
We don't really need
the baby, do we?

I wonder if the baby will work here in the zoo one day, looking after the animals.

Then the baby might get eaten by a tiger.

I wonder if the
baby will be a
sailor and take
us out in a boat.

We could sail
round the world,
but I think I should
be the captain.

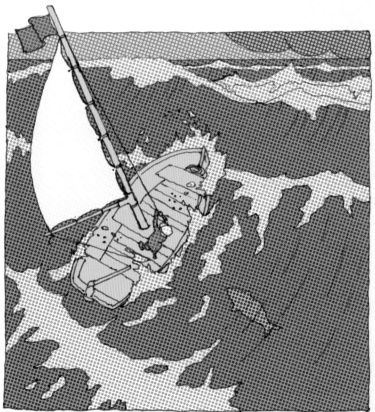

Perhaps the baby
will work here
in the bank when
it is older.

Well, that would
be very good.
Then it could
give me lots
of money.

Mrs Anderson's baby was sick
all over their new carpet.

They always need people
to work in the park,
so that is something
the baby could do
later on.

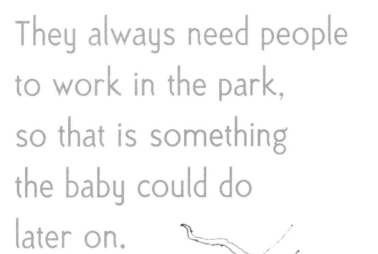

I don't think the
baby could ever
collect up all
these leaves.

The baby could
be a doctor or
a nurse when it
grows up.

I hope the baby
doesn't look
after me if
I'm ill.

When is the baby coming, Mummy?
I want to see the baby.

It won't be long now.
The baby is being as quick as it can.

Grandad, we're going to
see the baby now.
Maybe it will be Susan or Peter.
Maybe it will be good at cooking
and it will sail on the seven seas
and work in the garden or
the zoo or the bank.

Grandad,
the baby will
be our baby.
We're going to
love the baby,
aren't we?